"Through the ups and downs, routines and regimens of our daily existence, we can become complacent, even bored, with life. But God never meant for life to be boring. And in *One Month to Live,* Kerry and Chris Shook remind us of the true depth and meaning that God has in store for each of our lives. No matter where you are in your walk with God, this book will reveal to you a fresh and much-needed perspective. And at the end of this thirty-day journey, you will discover exactly what it means to truly live—daily…creatively…passionately!"

—ED YOUNG, senior and founding pastor of Fellowship Church and
    author of *Outrageous, Contagious Joy*

"Too many people live with regrets, missed opportunities, and dormant dreams. You don't have to be one of them. Your life will be different if you apply the transformational principles in Kerry and Chris Shook's *One Month to Live.*"

—CRAIG GROESCHEL, founding pastor of Lifechurch.tv and author of
    Confessions of a Pastor

"*One Month to Live* by Kerry and Chris Shook will add value to the life of every person who reads it. The questions asked and the 'Make It Count Moments' in this book will stir your soul and inspire you to begin, today, to make the rest of your life more meaningful. What Kerry and Chris present in *One Month to Live* could be life altering."

—KEN BLANCHARD, author of *The One Minute Manager* and *Know*
    Can Do!

"If you want new urgency, fresh purpose, and a sharper focus for your life, then this book is for you. Read it and your future may be changed forever!"

—LEE STROBEL, author of *The Case for the Real Jesus*

"Regardless of where you are on your spiritual journey, *One Month to Live* will challenge you to passionately live the life you were made for and leave an eternal legacy."

—BILL HYBELS, best-selling author and senior pastor of Willow Creek Community Church

ONE MONTH TO *live*

ONE MONTH TO LIVE GUIDEBOOK
PUBLISHED BY WATERBROOK PRESS
12265 Oracle Boulevard, Suite 200
Colorado Springs, Colorado 80921

ISBN 978-0-30745-709-7

Published in the United States by WaterBrook Multnomah, an imprint of the Crown Publishing Group, a division of Random House Inc., New York.

WATERBROOK and its deer colophon are registered trademarks of Random House Inc.

Printed in the United States of America
2009

10 9 8 7 6 5 4 3

SPECIAL SALES
Most WaterBrook Multnomah books are available in special quantity discounts when purchased in bulk by corporations, organizations, and special-interest groups. Custom imprinting or excerpting can also be done to fit special needs. For information, please e-mail SpecialMarkets@WaterBrookMultnomah.com or call 1-800-603-7051.

Contents

How to Use This Guidebook 1

Introduction 3

Session 1: *Real Life* 5

Session 2: *Live Passionately* 25

Session 3: *Love Completely* 49

Session 4: *Learn Humbly* 73

Session 5: *Leave Boldly* 97

Session 6: *Living Like There's No Tomorrow* 121

Conclusion 136

How to Use This Guidebook

This guide to *One Month to Live* is designed to be used in three ways:

1. *Personal guide.* If you want to better understand the major concepts of the one-month-to-live lifestyle, you will profit greatly from a careful study of this material. Each session in the guidebook contains three sections for personal study and action: Engage, Explore, and Enact. If you read the background chapters in *One Month to Live,* which is strongly recommended, plan on investing one or two hours on each session.

The guidebook includes ample space for you to write your answers, comments, and questions. A special page—Journal Your Life—follows the conclusion of each session. This is a place for you to write any ideas, conclusions, challenges, and personal insights that you found meaningful in that week's material.

2. *One-on-one study.* This approach is for you and an accountability partner, and it may be your best way to get the most benefit from this guidebook. Each week, both you and your partner can accomplish your individual study of the session material. Then you can get together to review the content and your answers to the questions. You can also encourage each other to press on and complete the thirty-day challenge.

3. *Small group discussion guide.* No one is meant to live the Christian life alone. We strongly urge you to join a small group—or start one yourself—to study this material in community. During the thirty-day challenge, you will rely on the

encouragement, support, and prayer of your teammates. Each session of the *One Month to Live Guidebook* includes questions for group use—Small Group Discussion. These discussions will be most rewarding if every participant completes his or her personal study of the session material prior to the small group meeting. You may also want to use the *One Month to Live Small Group DVD* as a discussion prompt for your group.

The end of each session includes information on the suggested background reading for the next session.

The *One Month to Live Guidebook* is designed for a six- to ten-session time frame (sessions 2–5 include bonus material and questions for those wanting to follow the ten-week track). However, if completing the study takes you even longer—personally or as a small group—by all means invest the time you need. We have found, however, that there are definite benefits for completing your study of the material in a shorter rather than longer time frame.

Before you begin each study, commit your time to God. Ask the Holy Spirit to illumine your mind, guide your heart, and energize your spirit as you read each section and answer each question.

Above all, please adapt this guidebook so that it truly works for *you*. This guidebook is your invitation to know God and His ways better, to learn about the calling on your life, and to become more effective in building a lasting legacy.

Introduction

One day while speaking to a large crowd, Jesus told a sobering parable. It concerned a rich farmer who had been blessed with a great harvest. An entrepreneurial kind of guy, he decided to think big. Here's how the story played out—as Jesus told it:

> Then he [the farmer] said, "Here's what I'll do: I'll tear down my barns and build bigger ones. Then I'll gather in all my grain and goods, and I'll say to myself, Self, you've done well! You've got it made and can now retire. Take it easy and have the time of your life!"
>
> Just then God showed up and said, "Fool! Tonight you die. And your barnful of goods—who gets it?"
>
> That's what happens when you fill your barn with Self and not with God (Luke 12:18–21, MSG).

As He does better than anyone who ever set foot on our planet, Jesus nailed it: We need to live in such a way that if our time here comes to an abrupt end, we will be ready to enter heaven and meet God with no regrets.

We wrote the book *One Month to Live* to show how looking at life from a different perspective can help us see what it means to fill our barns with God—not with Self.

Now, in the *One Month to Live Guidebook,* you have the opportunity to take a deeper look into where you're headed with your life and, where necessary, to make the changes that will someday bring you to heaven with barns overflowing with the good works that God gave you to accomplish.

None of us knows how much time we have—thirty minutes, thirty days, thirty years. But when we are living a passionate, obedient lives—full of love for God and others—it really doesn't matter. Jesus said, "I have come that they may have life, and have it to the full" (John 10:10). That's what we're after! May God give you new insights into how to find and live such a life through your study and discussion of this guidebook.

Kerry

Chris

Real Life

Related background reading for this session: Introduction in One Month to Live.

We all hope it never happens, but what if it did?

The doctor looks at you with a serious expression and says, "I have some very unfortunate news. Your condition is irreversible. You do not have that long to live."

"Well, how long?" you ask, your eyes filling with tears. You are in shock. You never believed this could happen to you.

"I would estimate a month or so."

At that moment everything would change. Depending on how you chose to face facts, each day would be either a precious gift or a descent into fear.

And, thanks be to God, the same choice faces us every day. When we realize how unpredictable yet precious life is, we can decide to make every moment count. That's what this guide is for—to show us how to live *now* as though we only had one month to live.

Engage

One of the awesome responsibilities—and opportunities—of ministry is that we have been privileged to walk beside people who know that their time on earth is short. No doubt, some people do struggle terribly and become inconsolable. But the vast majority face their final days with increased joy and become radiantly alive!

> ∼ Most of them make radical changes as a result of their awareness of their terminal conditions. They take license to say what they really feel and do what they really want. They ask for forgiveness and forgive others. They no longer think only of themselves but reach out to those they love and let them know how much they mean. They take risks they would never have taken before and allow themselves to lay worry aside and gratefully accept each new day. They seem to gain a new clarity about their priorities, like their relationship with God and leaving legacies that will endure.
>
> Over the years of watching others live out their last days, I began to ask myself, *Why can't all of us live more like we're dying? Isn't that how we were meant to live in the first place? To discover what we're made for and to utilize our unique gifts in the limited amount of time we're given?* ∼ *

1. Why do you think many people facing death actually become more alive?

---

* Passages marked with the ∼ icon are excerpts from the book *One Month to Live*.

2. Have you ever been near someone, perhaps a family member or friend, who knew the time was short? If so, how did this person walk through the experience? How were you affected by this person's response?

3. Why might a Christian have a more positive response to news of impending death?

🙠 If their days were numbered, most people would want to spend their time carefully and deliberately. I haven't met anyone who knew their days were limited who wanted to catch up on television reruns and maybe spend a little more time reformatting their hard drive. It's not that these are bad pursuits. In fact, chores and mundane responsibilities are part of daily life. But if we knew we had one month to live, I suspect most of us would experience crystal clarity about how to prioritize our time. Certainly chores and duties have to be kept up on a daily basis, but even these can be connected to larger goals—communicating with our spouse, teaching our kids, or connecting with God. The mundane can become magnificent if we're plugged into each hour and each other. 🙠

4. How could the mundane become more magnificent in your life if you had more of a one-month-to-live mind-set?

5. What are some of the daily experiences, the "little things" in your life, that are your treasure and delight?

☙ If you knew you only had one month to live, certainly those remaining minutes, hours, and days would become your most precious commodity. Like a billionaire who suddenly discovers he's down to his last hundred dollars, you would immediately stop taking your time for granted and would be aware of how you spent every minute. You would want each of them to be rich with enjoyment, significance, and investment in others.…

Wouldn't you want to take more time to linger over a meal with your family? to inhale the rich aroma of a cup of coffee as you watch the sunrise through your kitchen window? to cheer your son at his basketball game? to read a meaningful book, poem, or passage of Scripture? to take a walk through the piney woods, listening to the birds chatter. ☙

6. Make a list of some activities you spend time on now that may be robbing you of time that could be invested more wisely.

7. Make another list of the half dozen or so activities or experiences that you absolutely must do soon, the kinds of things you would really miss if they were no longer available to you.

☞ Several terminally ill people I've known have told me that, ironically, they eventually felt relieved by their prognosis. By forcing them to slow down and make radical changes, their bodies provided something their souls had been craving for a long time. ☞

8. Are there some things your soul is craving? Listen in prayer to what God is saying to you about what is really important in your life.

Explore

⤳ Perhaps no place echoes with eternity quite like a cemetery.… The dates on some of the old monuments and grave markers in the Houston area where I live go back to the eighteen hundreds. My imagination launches me into the various stories the markers tell. I find myself pondering what life was like in 1823 or 1914.…

Looking at old tombstones, I can't help but recognize that entire lives are now reduced before me to two dates and one little dash. Some monuments include facts or sayings, Bible verses or poignant memorials, but each person's life really comes down to what transpired between those two dates. It comes down to what's in the dash. ⤳

1. Why do most people not think much about their "dash"?

2. In our culture death seems almost a taboo subject. Why do you think that is?

3. Among your relatives, friends, and acquaintances, are there people who seem especially concerned about their legacies? What about their lives are different from those who are not thinking about the end of their lives?

When you think about it, we don't have control over many things in life. We didn't get to decide where we were born, who our parents are, or which time period and culture we face. We don't get to decide the dates on our gravestone. We don't know when our time on this earth will be up. It could be next week or next year or decades away. Only God knows. Our lives are in His hands. But there is one thing we have a vast amount of control over. We get to decide how we're going to use our dash.

You get to choose how to spend that little dash of time between the two dates of your earthly existence. What are you spending yours on? Are you living the dash, knowing fully who you are and why you're here? Or dashing to live, hurriedly spending precious time chasing things that really don't matter to you? The psalmist prayed, "Teach us to number our days and recognize how few they are; help us to spend them as we should" (Psalm 90:12, TLB).

4. How do you feel about how you have "lived your dash" so far? Are there some things you want to change to make your life more focused?

↝ While many of the people I've known who are facing death make radical changes in order to die well, occasionally I meet some who change very little. It's not that they are unwilling to change. It's that they have lived so deliberately and so authentically that the news of the end of this life doesn't turn them upside down. Of course they grieve and struggle with the news. They ache for their families and the people they love. But they take comfort in knowing they have been living focused on what matters most to them: their relationships with the ones they love, their relationship with the God of the universe, and the fulfillment of their unique purpose on this earth. ↝

5. In your life now, how might you improve the state of your (a) relationships with those you love, (b) relationship with God, and (c) unique purpose on earth?

～ Wouldn't it be wonderful to spend your life so that if you discovered you only had a month to live, you wouldn't need to change a thing? What's holding you back? What are you waiting on? Repeatedly in Scripture, God reminds us that our lives are short compared to eternity. "Why, you do not even know what will happen tomorrow. What is your life? You are a mist that appears for a little while and then vanishes" (James 4:14).

Of course I'm not encouraging you simply to live for today. Most of us can't afford to quit our jobs overnight, say what we're really feeling all the time, or act on every spontaneous idea. This kind of a lifestyle seems selfish and wildly indulgent and may indicate that such a person doesn't believe there's anything beyond this life. But life is more than what we know of it on earth. Even as we engage ourselves in the present, we must think through the eternal impact of how we live....

Be brutally honest with yourself. *Your time on earth is limited. Shouldn't you start making the most of it?* If you knew you had one month to live, you would look at everything from a different perspective. Many of the things you do now that seem so important would immediately become meaningless. You would have total clarity about what matters most, and you wouldn't hesitate to be spontaneous and risk your heart. You wouldn't wait until tomorrow to do what you need to do today. The way you lived that month would be the way you wished you had lived your whole life. ～

Enact

With only a month to live, there are certain things we would need to take care of. The items that follow certainly are not exhaustive, but my hunch is that all of us would deal with these to some extent.

Let Go of Failure and Receive Forgiveness

✦ I have to admit my sins so I can be forgiven. I have to admit my failures so I can learn from them. "A man who refuses to admit his mistakes can never be successful. But if he confesses and forsakes them, he gets another chance" (Proverbs 28:13, TLB). When we admit our mess-ups, we get another chance. When we take responsibility for our failures and don't blame other people, God forgives and gives us the power to start over.

There's more: you must also release your guilt.... You may feel like you're so far off God's track for your life right now that you can never get back. You've made a lot of mistakes, a lot of selfish choices. You've let down a lot of people. You feel like your race has ended in a messy crash.

I have news for you: get ready for an amazing race. God says, "I still have a race for you to run!" ✦

1. We all have "sinned and fall short of the glory of God" (Romans 3:23). If you are wanting to get "cleaned up" for the next stage of your journey, this would be a good time to ask God for forgiveness of your sins and mistakes.

✦ To begin again we need to surrender to God's power. But surrender means yielding—giving ourselves over to His way of doing things. Jesus explained it this way: "If anyone would come after me, he must deny himself and take up his cross daily and follow me" (Luke 9:23). Jesus tells us to deny ourselves in order to find fulfillment....

This is just the opposite of what we hear every day in the world around us. We have to exchange mantras—from *satisfy* myself to *deny* myself.... Every day of my life, I come to the place where I fall on my face and say, "God, I can't do it. I give up." And God says, *Finally. I've been waiting for that. Now I can get involved and give you My power and My strength.*

When we give ourselves to God as the source of all the power in our lives, then we see results we could never attain on our own. ↝

2. In what areas of your life now do you really need God's power and strength?

Embrace Relationships

↝ If we knew we were facing only a few weeks to live, we would not want to die alone. We would want those we care about to know our truest selves, to know how grateful we are for them. We would want to give them our final heart messages. We would want to leave behind a relational legacy of enduring love and ongoing faith. ↝

3. Who needs to hear you say, "I love you"? Or who needs to hear, "Will you forgive me?" Who would love to hear you say, "I forgive you"? Make a list and seize the opportunities.

Face Fear

☙ The Bible tells us that perfect love casts out fear (1 John 4:18). It doesn't say that perfection casts out fear or that perfect love ensures our success the way we want it. When we know God's love, the care and compassion of a loving Father who wants us to trust Him, then we can let go. His love is so much greater than our fears....

It's certainly not like we can flip a switch and turn off our fear or push a button and be happy. We may not be able to control what we feel, but we definitely can control what we do with those emotions—how they affect our thoughts and behavior. Since our feelings can fluctuate based on our mood, circumstances, physical health, and other factors, it becomes essential that we go back to our primary source, our spiritual connection to God.... The New Testament says, "For God gave us a spirit not of fear but of power and love and self-control" (2 Timothy 1:7, ESV). If I'm connected to my Creator with constant conversation and constant confession, then He'll give me the power and self-control I need. ☙

4. What do you fear in your life? What does God want you to do about those fears?

Redeem Failure

Loss and failure, when viewed with humility, can become stepping stones to success. God loves to take the weak and the broken pieces of our lives and show us His creativity in redeeming failures.

    We've all heard stories about celebrities and successful businesspeople who failed miserably early in their careers, only to wander "accidentally" into new ventures for which they were naturally suited. Henry Ford wasn't a good businessman (he went bankrupt five times), but he was a visionary engineer. Oprah was fired from her job as a television reporter before launching her now-successful show and far-reaching media empire....

    While struggling to invent an electrical light, Thomas Alva Edison declared, "I have not failed. I've just found ten thousand ways that don't work."...

    In fact, if we looked at the lives of every person, both historical and contemporary, whom we consider "successful," we wouldn't find an absence of failure, fear, or pain. Instead we would find the common denominators of perseverance and purpose converging to motivate and inspire these achievers to move forward....

    Everyone who has succeeded has also failed many times.... We need that same persistence to keep going. The greatest power we need in our lives is the power to begin again.

5. What specific challenge are you currently facing in life that would benefit from applying a greater sense of your purpose and more perseverance?

~ If you're going to have the power to begin again, you must learn from your losses. The key to not only knowing this lesson but owning and activating it is to humbly admit our failures….

When one of my children fails a math test or fails to obey curfew, I don't stop loving him or her. And depending on the circumstances and why and how they failed, it can be an incredible teaching moment.

Similarly, God loves to redeem our failures, to transform our mistakes—whether rebellious or well intended—into part of His plan and our ultimate purpose….

[Jesus] just looks with compassion right into your heart. He sees the guilt and the regret and the shame. But He does say something to you. He says that because of the power of His love for you, failure is never final. Because of the power of the Cross—the ultimate sacrifice producing power over death—our weaknesses and failures and selfishness can never keep us down. Failure is never fatal. We have the God of the second chance, and He wants to give us the power to begin again. ~

6. Is there an area or two of your life where it would be great to "begin again"? Now's the time! The "One Month" Challenge is a time to renew your hope in big dreams.

Looking Ahead

During the next four sessions, we will carefully study the four big ideas that make up the foundation for the one-month-to-live lifestyle:

- *Live passionately*—holding nothing back in seeking all that God wants for us.
- *Love completely*—pouring ourselves into making life better for those we love and influence.
- *Learn humbly*—becoming wise in our understanding of God and His perfect ways.
- *Leave boldly*—obediently doing for God the things that matter now, as well as building a legacy for eternity.

1. What do you hope will be the outcome of investing your time and attention in the thirty-day challenge?

↬ We were created for so much more than punching buttons and scrolling screens. We were created for a grand adventure! God designed us to take great risks and face huge challenges, to accomplish mighty goals that will have a lasting impact. ↫

At the end of each session of the *One Month to Live Guidebook,* you will have the opportunity to journal your reflections and insights from the just-completed study. We will prompt you with a thought or question, but more importantly we encourage you to use the journal as your personal place to creatively record your ideas and impressions.

Journal Your Life

Based on your study of this session of the guide, record your thoughts related to real life. How is God leading you to make the most of your one-month-to-live experience?

_____

_____

_____

_____

_____

_____

Small Group Discussion

Take a few minutes to get acquainted by sharing names and other information with the group.

1. If you had only *one day to live,* what would be the *one thing* you would do for sure?
2. What drew you to attend this one-month-to-live small group?
3. What do you hope to gain from this group during the coming sessions?
4. What are some of the changes you would make if you really had only a month to live?
5. What are the things in daily life—even the good things—that can take our attention away from accomplishing the goals and dreams God has given us?
6. In the book *One Month to Live* we read, "Life is more than what we know of it on earth." What would you say is the "more" referred to here?
7. Drawing on experiences of group members and people they know, share some stories of people who have grasped a one-month-to-live mind-set. What is different about these men and women? How do they maintain such a focus on what is really important?
8. Psalm 90:12 reads, "Teach us to number our days and recognize how few they are; help us to spend them as we should" (TLB). How does an understanding of the scope of eternity help us clarify our goals on earth?

Wrap up with prayer for one another.

Next Session: Live Passionately

Before the next session:

- Review days 2–8 in the book *One Month to Live*.
- Read and answer the Engage, Explore, and Enact sections in session 2 of this guide.
- Visit www.OneMonthToLive.com to learn more about how to live your life to the fullest.

Live Passionately

Related background reading for this session: Days 2–8 in One Month to Live.

Without passion, not much of value happens. A significant first step in developing a one-month-to-live perspective is to understand the role of passion in a successful life. Too many people have settled for a passionless life. That certainly is not an existence that God designed for any of us! Of all people, those who follow Jesus should be marked by an intense interest and involvement in all of life.

In this session we will learn what it means to "leave it all on the field" and *live passionately.*

Engage

☞ Just as the roller-coaster ride passes in a flash, our lives on this earth are temporal and finite. It's a natural part of being human; we're born, and eventually our bodies will die. Instead of finding this depressing or paralyzing, if you're willing to face and own this truth about life—that it will end as you know it here—then you can be truly free. Instead of limiting us, our mortality can consistently remind us to be all we were made to be. ☙

1. Is it difficult for you to think about your own mortality? Why or why not?

2. Why is facing the reality of life—including the fact that as Solomon wrote in Ecclesiastes, there is "a time to be born and a time to die" (3:2)—a wise thing to do?

❧ Often we're tempted to play it safe and settle for far less than we were made for. I know so many people whose favorite day of the week is *Someday*. Countless people in every stage of life say, "Someday I'm going to go for all that life has to offer." "When I retire, then I'm going to enjoy life." "Someday I'm really going to live for God and get my act together. I'll start loving my family better." "When I make enough money, then I'm really going to spend more time with my kids." "Someday when my schedule slows down, then I'm going to get involved at church." "When I have more time, then I'll focus on being more spiritual."

Someday. One day. When. If. Then it's over. When are we going to wake up and realize *this is life*? ❧

3. Why do you think many people do not get around to doing the things they know are most important?

4. In your own experience, what are the things that hold you back from pursuing all that life has to offer?

❧ As I look at life from a God-level perspective, I begin to understand that the life of faith that everyone else calls ridiculous is the only reasonable way to live.

The world says, "Don't be ridiculous; be reasonable. Don't stand out. Don't take risks; play it safe, and make security and comfort your primary goals in life."…

God did not design us simply to stand by and watch life pass as we wonder why we aren't more fulfilled. God created us to take risks in faith and to conquer the giants that paralyze us with fear. ❧

5. Why does the world place so much emphasis on comfort and security?

6. In your life, what are some of the risks of faith God has asked you to take? What has been the outcome of taking those risks—or not taking them?

↜ As difficult and frightening as your life may be right now, God is still there. He cares about you beyond what you can understand or even imagine. If you knew you only had a month to live, wouldn't you want to leave the safe ride behind and get on the one that makes your heart come alive? Wouldn't you want to be on the ride that fulfills you—with joy, with fear, with a level of engagement that allows you to savor each moment? ↝

Explore

What are the building blocks of a life filled with passion? Certainly one of the most passionate men in the Bible is King David, who took on a giant with a slingshot but also wrote some of Scripture's most beautiful poetry. David also had a huge failure that threatened to derail his life for good. We can learn a great deal about passionate living by taking a closer look at King David.

    ✒ We're to be like the teenage boy who stepped forward to challenge the giant Goliath in the ultimate death match. Despite all the thousands of men in the Israelite army, David was the only person who had the courage to face the giant. King Saul should have been the one to fight the Philistine giant, but he had long ago stopped following God with reckless abandon and was now playing it safe. Saul told David, "Don't be ridiculous! How can a kid like you fight with a man like him? You are only a boy and he has been in the army *since* he was a boy!" (1 Samuel 17:33, TLB).

    When you think about it for a moment, you realize Saul was right in his assessment.... Saul and the army of Israel were operating on the basis of reason. David was operating on the basis of faith. When you're operating on the basis of reason, all you can see is how big your giants are. If you're operating in faith, all you can see is how small your giants are compared to God.

    The one thing that separated David from the thousands who were there that day was ridiculous faith. ✒

1. Why do you think David had "ridiculous faith"?

Faith and Dreams

Faith and dreams intertwine. A life of passion involves holding on to the reality of your dreams when circumstances offer minimal or no hope. Another word for that is faith.

       A dream is something that calls to us, something that may seem impossible or crazy but tastes sweeter and more fulfilling than we ever could have imagined.

For most of us, though, fulfilling our dreams rarely goes smoothly....

Everyday life has a way of wearing down the dreams of our youth and deflating the hope of seeing them come to pass. We get frostbitten by the bitter cold of disappointment, delay, and deferment. Instead of dreaming big and believing that God can accomplish great things through us, we go into survival mode and put our dreams on ice.

2. What are some of the dreams God has given you? If you can't remember any, take some time alone with God and let Him remind you of dreams you may have forgotten.

       I believe God wants to thaw out that frozen dream that He placed in your heart. He wants to rescue you from an ordinary existence and bring your dream back to life! The Psalmist said, "Taste and see that the LORD is good" (Psalm 34:8). I have found there is nothing tastier and more fulfilling than discovering and following the dream God has planted in your heart....

So how do you know if a dream is really from God or if it's just an idea that popped into your head? For one thing, God's dream will never go against His Word, because His will never contradicts His Word. If the desire you have goes against God's Word, it's not His dream. ☙

3. Looking back on your life, have you had dreams that you now know were not from God? How did you determine that a dream(s) had to be abandoned?

☙ Paul told us the secret to determining if a dream is from God when he said, "God…is able to do far more than we would ever dare to ask or even dream of—infinitely beyond our highest prayers, desires, thoughts, or hopes" (Ephesians 3:20, TLB). God's dream will rise to the top while everything else will melt away.…

If a dream is from God, it will be so big in your life that you can't do it on your own. If you can accomplish it by yourself, no faith is required. The Bible says, "Without faith it is impossible to please God" (Hebrews 11:6). So if a dream is from God, it will rise to the top because it will be so big you can't do it alone. ☙

The Opposition

Life would be difficult enough without a huge opposing force that constantly attempts to derail God's dreams for you. The reality is that you have an Enemy who is fighting against you.

❧ The Bible says God has a plan for our lives, an intricately designed, grand plan. But Satan also has a plan for our lives. Nowhere is the contrast between these conflicted purposes expressed more clearly than in this passage: "The thief's purpose is to steal and kill and destroy. My purpose is to give life in all its fullness" (John 10:10, NLT). God's purpose is to give you a dream. Satan's purpose is to steal the dream....

Satan knows the dream starts in your heart, so he's committed to wounding your heart, taking it out of action, and freezing your God-given dream with soul-numbing cold. He constantly bombards you with messages that say you can't do it, that you'll never amount to anything of substance. ❧

4. Do you think Satan has stolen a dream from you? If you are not sure, ask God in prayer to reveal the truth. The great news is that our God has overcome the Enemy!

The Power Behind Passion

❧ Do you ever feel powerless in life? Many people tell me that the number one reason they don't try to change is because they feel powerless to alter the combined force of all the circumstances in their lives. Maybe you have a habit you feel powerless to break. Or maybe you have a problem in a relationship, and you've tried everything to restore it, yet it's still falling apart. Or maybe an issue at work is draining your energy and your creativity, and you can't see a solution....

People who know their lives will soon be over tend to feel a desperate urge to change. But a desperation to change is not enough. In order to sustain the changes, we have to be connected to a power source beyond ourselves—a power source that never wavers, flickers, or leaves us in the dark. We have to move from willpower to the real power that comes from a connection to our Creator....

You have...limitless power available to you each and every day.... In Ephesians, Paul says, "I pray that you will begin to understand how incredibly great his power is to help those who believe him. It is that same mighty power that raised Christ from the dead" (1:19–20, TLB). He'll give you all the power you need for the one-month-to-live lifestyle. ⌒

5. In your experience, what helps you connect to the power of God? What hinders you?

⌒ Some people talk about spiritual growth and how they can stimulate it in their lives, but to gain the power to change, what we need to seek is not spiritual growth but spiritual health. Healthy things grow, so you don't need to focus on spiritual growth during this thirty-day challenge. Instead, focus on spiritual health.... The key to spiritual health is maintaining a strong relationship with your Creator. If you are connected to your Creator, you will grow like you've never grown before, and you'll experience real power to make lasting changes. ⌒

6. In what ways do you want to become more spiritually healthy during your thirty-day challenge?

Enact

Clearly passion is critical to living the life God intends for us. But what if the passion is gone from your life? How can you reenergize and activate your enthusiasm and drive?

Your Own Mask First

☞ Depending on how frequently you fly, you may know [the oxygen mask] drill by heart. It's part of every flight attendant's monologue covering safety procedures at the beginning of a flight. The rationale for such instruction is obvious: you can't help anyone if you've passed out from lack of oxygen yourself.

However, these words also contain a powerful spiritual truth. If you're going to make the most of your time on earth, living a no-regrets lifestyle, then you need to engage fully with those around you.… If you're not healthy spiritually, physically, emotionally, and relationally, how can you move beyond yourself and invest in others?…

Loving ourselves is a biblical command. Jesus Himself said this in identifying the greatest commandments: "'Love the Lord your God with all your heart, soul, and mind.' This is the first and greatest commandment. The second most important is similar: 'Love your neighbor as much as you love yourself'" (Matthew 22:37–39, TLB). Most of us…miss the last part of this message: we are to love our neighbor *as much as we love ourselves.*...

In fact, until you learn how to love yourself, you can never really learn to love and care for others the way God wants you to. ☙

1. Do you find it difficult to put your own "oxygen mask" on first and properly love yourself? List details to support your answer.

2. How might you love God better? love others better?

Physical Health: A Well-Maintained Temple

☙ How you treat your body is an area where the reality of the one-month-to-live lifestyle extends far beyond a few weeks.

Whether you have thirty days or thirty years left, you should realize that how you treat your body has a direct and lasting impact on the quality of life you enjoy. Giving up exercise, eating more desserts, and staying out late might seem great for a few days, but we've all experienced those slumps where our energy level plummeted because we neglected ourselves. Our bodies require sleep, exercise, clean air, water, and quality nourishment. ~

3. What are some ways you could improve your physical health and strength?

~ To be healthy physically, we must be healthy spiritually and listen to what God says about our bodies. In a letter to the church at Corinth, Paul wrote, "Have you forgotten that your body is the temple of the Holy Spirit, who lives in you…, and that you are not the owner of your own body?" (1 Corinthians 6:19, Phillips).

I often see two extremes when it comes to the concepts people have about their bodies. The first is, some people worship the temple. They don't worship the One *in* the temple but the temple itself. These are the people who spend countless hours trying to look better.… But here's the crucial problem: whenever you worship the temple, your body—something that's guaranteed to change—you'll feel insecure. The other extreme is just as harmful—people who trash the temple. They neglect their bodies completely and couldn't care less about their overall health.…

If you knew God was coming to your house for dinner tonight, wouldn't you want to pick up, clean, and prepare for His visit? You need to realize that God lives in your house right now. He lives in you. Your body is the temple of God, and that's why it's so important to take care of yourself and cultivate physical energy. ~

4. What is the best action you could take to improve maintenance of your temple of God?

Emotional Health: Feeling Good About How You Feel

So many people function according to how they feel. They work hard when they feel like it. They go to church when they feel like it. They act lovingly toward their wife or husband when they feel like it. They work at being a better parent when they want to feel better about themselves, not when their children need to feel loved.

A huge part of maturing, of growing up, is learning to acknowledge and experience our emotions without being controlled by them....

Don't let the course of your life be dictated by your emotions. Feel what you feel, but then do what God wants you to do.

5. In what environments or situations are you most influenced by feelings? Why is this?

Relational Health: Connected to Others God's Way

~ The whole reason we put the oxygen mask on ourselves first is so we can breathe in and get healthy and help someone else find God's oxygen.... Just as God created us as eternal beings in temporal bodies, He designed us to live in concert with others. We were not meant to be self-sufficient and independent so that we can isolate ourselves and avoid other people. ~

6. Why are relationships so prominent when we seriously evaluate our priorities?

A Passion for Greatness

~ What keeps us clinging to our own efforts instead of risking the greatness that God directs us toward? For many of us, it's the loss of control. We think that if we really let go and allow God to catch and direct us, we'll end up spending our lives like a prison sentence, doing something we hate. But that couldn't be further from the truth! God has created each one of us to fulfill a purpose, and He has designed us uniquely to accomplish it. He's planted eternity in our hearts along with seeds of greatness that can only grow through our willingness to serve.

What does letting go look like? From my experience, it often involves patience and looking for God's hand in places we might not expect. God rarely conforms to our timetables or does things in a neat, linear way from our human and limited perspective....

Each and every day I have to come to the place where I realize I can't control everything in my life, and I have to let go and surrender to God. He always catches me, and that's when I feel His peace and strength in the stressful moments of life.

7. In order to live a passionate life, what must you stop seeking to control? After you've written your list, ask the Lord for the power and strength to surrender control of each item.

Journal Your Life

Based on your study of this session of the guide, record your thoughts related to living passionately. What has God placed on your heart that stirs your deepest longings?

_____

_____

_____

_____

_____

Small Group Discussion

Take a few minutes to review the journey of each group member since you were last together.

1. How would you define a life of passion?
2. What are some of the actions or experiences that people say they will do "someday"?
3. The Bible says Jesus is the vine and we are the branches. What do you think that means today? Share examples with one another.
4. The book *One Month to Live* says of God's pruning, "The pruning process is always painful, but it's always productive." What's been your experience when God prunes you?
5. God is a giver of dreams. What dreams has He given you?
6. What obstacles to fulfilling your dreams have you encountered?
7. *One Month to Live* states, "The only way to risk greatness is to trust God with all areas of your life." How can we go about trusting God more completely?
8. Fear of failure, or actual failure, derails many people from lives of greatness. Why do we fear failure so much? What can we do to move beyond such fear?
9. What examples of "ridiculous faith" would you like to share, from your life or the lives of others?

Wrap up with prayer for one another.

Next Session: Love Completely

Before the next session:

- Review days 9–15 in the book *One Month to Live.*
- Read and answer the Engage, Explore, and Enact sections in session 3 of this guide.
- Visit www.OneMonthToLive.com to learn more about how to live your life to the fullest.

Bonus Small Group Discussion

If your group wants to spend more time (perhaps an additional session) exploring the topic of living passionately, here are some additional excerpts from *One Month to Live* as well as questions for personal meditation and group discussion.

The Time of Your Life

1. Is it possible to manage time? Should we even try? How we use our precious hours and days will influence dramatically our ability to focus our passion in pursuit of our dreams.

How often do we hear and use the *b* word? *We're really busy.* Can you think of the last time you asked a friend how she was doing, and she said,

"Great. Things are really moving slowly. I have plenty of time to get every-thing done and spend quality time with my family and friends"?...

Time once spent cannot be reclaimed. Once an hour, minute, or moment is over, it's gone forever. However, we can redeem the remaining time we have. We can reconsider our God-given purpose and the eternal legacy we want to leave behind and allow them to guide our schedule moving forward. How do we refocus? The only way you and I can make the most of our remaining time is to spend each day in such a way that we leave behind a worthwhile legacy on this earth. In his letter to the church at Corinth, Paul wrote, "Companions as we are in this work with you, we beg you, please don't squander one bit of this marvelous life God has given us" (2 Corinthians 6:1, MSG). ❧

2. Why does everyone seem so busy these days?

3. Where do you think most people waste time?

❧ Jack Groppel, a peak-performance coach for many professional athletes, celebrities, and corporate CEOs, says time management is really energy man-agement....

It almost seems like a natural law of physics. When we increase our energy and level of engagement, we multiply our time. You can work eighteen-hour days and yet not be effective. In fact, it's probably detrimental overall, because you'll lose your creativity and health and eventually burn out. Most of us would agree that workaholism stems from poor energy management. ❧

4. Do you agree or disagree with Jack Groppel's conclusion that time management is really energy management? Elaborate on your answer.

True Productivity

❧ One of the challenges for most of us is what I call the productivity paradox. We're conditioned to believe that in order for our time to be worthwhile, we must have something to show for it. We produce something—another report, a new document, a better system, an improved product. Many people I know feel pressured to produce—even during their vacation and free time! They can't enjoy just relaxing by the pool or going for a walk or sleeping late, because they don't have anything to show for it.

The result is that we all need downtime to rest and to worship, to still ourselves before God, to think about our lives and to listen to His voice. The paradox is that we may not have anything to show for these truly productive moments. There is great freedom in learning to operate with an eternal perspective and not just by the watch on our wrist. A regular time of rest and recovery, a sabbath, is essential in our schedules. We need to become attuned to a greater measure of time than mere clocks and calendars. 🖘

5. Can you relate to the productivity paradox? Do you experience this in your life now? Explain.

6. What does *sabbath* mean to you?

7. Are you able to set aside downtime with God?

8. Do you feel you are able to find time to rest and relax so that you are restored? If not, what needs to change so you can get needed rest?

↝ In short, we're designed to require rest and to crave beauty. Even our Creator rested and observed a Sabbath. None of us would presume to be more productive than God, yet we often act as if we can't afford to stop, to pause, to still ourselves and rest at a soul level. ↝

The Power of Priorities

↝ Obviously, our priorities contribute powerfully to how we perceive time and how we spend it. We all have the same number of minutes in a day. There's nothing you or I can do to increase the length of a day to twenty-five hours, let alone the thirty or forty hours we might need in order to catch up. Bottom line, we're all stuck with twenty-four hours. How you invest those hours, however, can determine the difference between a sense of contentment, because you know you're doing exactly what you were made for, and a sense of regret. If you want to live with no regrets, then you may need to inventory your life and see how you've been spending your time. ↝

9. What success have you had in making sure your time is invested in priorities instead of wasted on activities that ultimately won't matter? If possible, gather more ideas from a friend or your small group.

☛ Make the most of your time by applying your energy to the areas that are your ongoing priorities. Keep in mind the legacy you want to leave behind—in the work you do, through the relationships you keep, and by the way you spend each day. We were not designed to be slaves to time. We were created to be active and present in the lives we've been given. Make the most of your time by spending it on a legacy that will last long after your time on earth has ended. ☛

10. What is the legacy you would like to be remembered for?

11. What barriers—if any—stand in the way of fulfilling your legacy?

Love Completely

Related background reading for this session: Days 9–15 in One Month to Live.

What would life be like without love? We know that beyond the cliché, in a real sense, love does "make the world go round." So why do we have so much trouble loving—and receiving love—in the ways that bring glory to God and great satisfaction to us? What are the secrets to loving without reservation, to letting our hearts flow with genuine affection, concern, and care for others?

Engage

God designed us to be in relationship both vertically with Him and horizontally with the people around us. Even though we may have a deep desire to connect with our families, friends, and communities, we've all experienced some of the messiness of relating to others. Expectations, disappointments, betrayals, hurts, lies, misunderstandings—there are so many obstacles to loving other people and being loved by them. But we were created for relationships, and if we only had one month left, we would be more concerned about them than ever before. ❧

1. Why is it so important to love completely in our relationships?

2. With relationships so crucial to human happiness, why do people so often neglect them?

❧ When all is said and done, relationships are all that really matter. It doesn't matter how much money we have, where we live, or how many beautiful toys we've collected. None of these can comfort us, console us, cry with us, or love us. Our investment in the people we care about is the only legacy that has the power to endure beyond our lifetime....

Love can't be bought, but it definitely carries a price, and it's called sacrifice. Love always means risking pain. Even in the best relationships, there's a haunting sense of potential loss—if nothing else, the possibility that the other person will die someday, leaving us alone. ❧

3. In your experiences, what are some of the "price tags" associated with loving others?

The Greatest Love

If we're going to love other people, to endure the heartaches as well as to celebrate the sharing of lives, then we will need a greater love than our own. We need to experience the fullness of God's love for us in order to die to our selfish desires and give freely to others....

The greatest sacrifice of love in history occurred in Christ's death on the cross. God allowed His only Son to become mortal—Word made flesh—and then to endure the most excruciatingly painful and publicly humiliating death possible: crucifixion. God's love for us is truly incomprehensible. Our love has limits, but God's love has none. It's completely unconditional, no strings attached....

Your problem is not that you don't love God enough. It's that you don't understand how much He loves you. If you could grasp just a little bit of how much God loves you, you'd surrender all areas of your life to Him. God would have given up His Son to come to this earth and die on the cross if you had been the only one on this earth.

4. Why is it difficult to love another person more than you feel loved by God?

5. In your life—in addition to your salvation experience—give examples of how God has loved you unconditionally.

⁓ The deepest place in the ocean is the Mariana Trench, at more than 36,000 feet. It's almost seven miles deep, and we can go down only 130 feet! Even if we use submersibles, most of the ocean is too deep and vast to be explored.

God's love is the same. Usually we just splash around on the surface, but He offers us a whole other level of depth in life. If we only had one month to live, I bet most of us would finally venture into deeper water, realizing that the only way we can be at peace is to confess our sins and experience the forgiveness and mercy He so freely gives. ⁓

6. What might it take for you to discover a whole new depth of God's love?

Explore

There is one word, perhaps more than any other, that is the perfect synonym for true love: *forgiveness*. The importance of forgiveness in our relationships was made very clear by Jesus when He said, "For if you forgive men when they sin against you, your heavenly Father will also forgive you. But if you do not forgive men their sins, your Father will not forgive your sins" (Matthew 6:14–15).

Until you experience the fullness of God's grace and forgiveness, you'll never be able to fully forgive others. You'll never be at peace and see the vision He has for you and your life. You'll never experience the blessings He wants to pour out on you. Forgiveness is not pretending that you weren't really hurt. It's not making light of the offense. Forgiveness is not a shallow experience. Forgiveness means diving deep into honesty and truthfully saying, "What you did hurt me deeply, but I choose to forgive you by God's power."

1. What's been your experience with forgiveness? Have you found forgiving others difficult or not? List reasons or examples for your answer.

The Bible gives…some great reasons to forgive.

The first is that Christ commands it. If you've committed your life to knowing and following Him, forgiveness is not an option. Paul wrote plainly to "forgive as the Lord forgave you" (Colossians 3:13). Throughout the Scriptures, forgiveness is not a suggestion. If you want to follow Jesus, it's a commandment. As difficult and emotionally challenging as it may be, we all have to practice forgiveness....

Likewise, if you try to live without forgiving, you won't survive. It is essential that we forgive for our own sakes; otherwise we'll drown in bitterness. The deeper you allow yourself to go into the ocean of resentment, the more you'll feel the pressure and the stress. Eventually the pressure will become so intense that your relationships, joy, and health will be crushed. Medical and psychological research reveal that bitterness and resentment have devastating effects. 〜

2. Have you known someone who just could not forgive someone else for a past hurt? What were the effects of such unforgiveness?

〜 We don't feel like forgiving people who hurt us, but that's okay. Forgiveness is not about what we feel. We forgive because we make a conscious decision and say to God, "I choose to forgive them by Your power because You command me to and because it's for my own good." Then five minutes later, when the hurt comes back to our minds, we can repeat this prayer, as many times as needed. Someone once wisely observed that to forgive is to set a prisoner free and to discover the prisoner was you. 〜

3. Why do we often have to forgive a person over and over for the same offense?

If it doesn't feel right to forgive someone repeatedly, we need to remember what Jesus said about this issue:

> Then Peter came to Jesus and asked, "Lord, how many times shall I forgive my brother when he sins against me? Up to seven times?"
>
> Jesus answered, "I tell you, not seven times, but seventy-seven times" (Matthew 18:21–22).

In other words, according to Jesus, there is no cap on the number of times we should forgive someone. We shouldn't keep count.

Relational Challenges

We all know it can be a steep climb from where we are to where we actually want to be. From my experience and the experiences of those I've counseled, it seems there are three mountains that generally prevent unity in relationships.

The first is what I call the mountain of misunderstanding. Most relationships don't have the power to climb over this first summit, and misconceptions and altercations quickly pile up as high as Pikes Peak. In the beginning of a relationship, everything seems so positive. You're climbing a smooth trail together, close beside each other, and then—*wham!*—you're faced with a big boulder of misunderstanding that seems to throw you both off course....

Another mountain that we must climb in any relationship is what I call the "me first" attitude. It's just human nature to say, "I'll meet your needs but only if you meet my needs first." Whether it's my kids fighting over who gets to ride shotgun in the car or my desire to control the television remote, we all would like to get what we want without thinking about what those around us need....

The third and final peak in this rocky range is the most deadly—the mountain of mistakes. Just as we have misunderstandings and the desire to put ourselves first, we all have faults, and we mess up. Many relationships are forever abandoned on the mountain of mistakes. Every one of us has been hurt by someone else's actions or words. It's easy when you're wounded in a relationship to fortify yourself and refuse to go any farther on this trail because the mountain is just too steep. ☞

4. In your life, what are the root causes of most misunderstandings?

5. Why is selfishness such a persistent problem in relationships?

6. How do you react when someone hurts your feelings? What is good and bad about this reaction?

Relational First Aid

↜ The Bible reveals strategies for keeping relational mountains small and manageable. In order to persevere and improve our relationships, we first must… "Accept one another, then, just as Christ accepted you, in order to bring praise to God" (Romans 15:7). One of our greatest problems in relationships is that we're always trying to change the people we're relating to. To accept others means that we stop trying to *change* them and we start trying to *understand* them.…

In conjunction with acceptance, we gain traction with loving action.… When you are inconsistent, telling others how important they are but never following through with loving actions, then the relationships will falter. The clarity and security your loving actions bring to the people around you can't be underestimated. ↜

7. How do you respond when someone tries to force you to change an attitude or behavior?

8. How do you respond when someone accepts and understands you—even when they know your flaws?

Enact

No question about it, loving others is not easy, which is why so many of us tend to postpone mending broken relationships.

> ⤚ We all know that sanding can be very useful when it comes to wood-working or finishing furniture. But if you take sandpaper and rub it against your skin, it doesn't feel good. It's abrasive and painful. There are certain people in our lives who are just as hurtful and annoying. They irritate us. They rub us the wrong way. They get under our skin.…
>
> The reality is that we're *all* sandpaper people. We all irritate other people at times, and that's part of God's plan for our lives. ⤚

1. How can being rubbed the wrong way by another person be used by God to benefit your life?

~ The Bible provides us with a guiding principle for getting along with sandpaper people and having a lasting impact in our relationships…. The first step in this process is to identify how other people bug you. While every individual is unique and every relationship special, I've found some categories helpful in thinking about our relational irritants….

- The first group reminds me of a measuring tape: these people always let you know that you don't quite measure up….

- Another type of person you may recognize is the hammer. Hammers tend to be as subtle as a freight train, pushing their agendas on others and forcing their way. Everyone walks on eggshells around a hammer, because you never know when the hammer's going to come down!…

- Next we come to those people who seem naturally gifted at cutting others down. In an argument, skill saws know just the thing to say that will hurt the most….

- Do you have any vise grips in your life? You know, people who get a grip on you and don't know when to let go? They are extra needy and usually squeeze the life out of those around them….

- In life's toolbox we also run across grinders, people with explosive personalities just waiting to go off and send the sparks flying….

- Related to the grinders are the axes, those who constantly cut a wide swath in their wake. They tend to be negative, always grumbling and looking for ways to tear down the hopes and plans of others….

- The hatchets usually take smaller chops but hold on to past hurts and grudges much longer. They don't know how to—you guessed it—bury the hatchet.

- Last but not least are the putty people. These are the people in your life who have no consistency, no backbone. Eager to please and always agreeable, they change like chameleons so that you never know who they really are or what they really think. ~

2. Which of these types of people—measuring tapes, hammers, skill saws, vise grips, grinders, axes, hatchets, putty people—bug you the most?

3. When you irritate others, which of these people types do you resemble?

↜ As uncomfortable or unsettling as we may find it, God intentionally places some people in our lives to rub us the wrong way, to smooth the rough edges of our character, so that we're more like Jesus.…

You get a whole new perspective on the difficult people in your life when you realize that not only has God placed them in your life for a reason but He has placed *you* in their lives for a reason. ↜

Sawdust and Planks

↜ Nobody I know is normal. You're not normal. I'm not normal. We're all unique. There is no one else in the world like you. Even though we're vastly different, we're all in the same toolbox. And instead of working together to build lasting relationships, as God intends, we're often tempted to criticize. It's always much easier for us to point out someone else's faults and flaws rather than look at our own.

Jesus talks about this in Matthew 7: "Why do you look at the speck of sawdust in your brother's eye and pay no attention to the plank in your own eye? How can you say to your brother, 'Let me take the speck out of your eye,' when all the time there is a plank in your own eye? You hypocrite, first take the plank out of your own eye, and then you will see clearly to remove the speck from your brother's eye" (verses 3–5).

We have sharp vision when it comes to finding the sawdust in everybody else's eyes. We see this little speck of sawdust, this fault, problem, sin, or character flaw in someone else's life, and we can't wait to point it out. ☞

4. Why are we so quick to point out the flaws in others?

5. Sometimes the flaws we are so quick to pounce on in others actually are reminding us of our own weaknesses. Have you observed that tendency in yourself?

❧ Notice that Jesus doesn't say to ignore the sawdust. Many people today think that whenever you point something out as sin, you're being judgmental. This isn't the case at all. We're to look at the sawdust in people's eyes and help heal them with Christ's power. Our role is not to judge but to be healing agents. ❧

6. Can you recall an instance where you pointed out someone's flaw or sin and you were well received? Is there an example where you were not well received?

❧ I've discovered that if I concentrate on my own shortcomings and let God give me the courage to face my own faults, character flaws, and mistakes, then I don't feel the urgency to help others see their specks. If I forget about trying to change everybody else and simply work on letting God change me, then the people in my life are much more open to me. ❧

Loving Connections

❧ Today we have satellite, teleconference, wireless, mobile, and hands-free communication abilities. While it seems you can reach anybody, anywhere, anytime, I wonder how often real connection occurs. Lines of communication are breaking down with alarming frequency—between husbands and wives, parents and teenagers, bosses and employees, co-workers, and friends. People talk all the time but rarely seem to hear each other's words, let alone their unspoken messages. ❧

7. Do you agree or disagree with the statement above: "People talk all the time but rarely seem to hear each others words." Why do you agree or disagree?

~ The people around us need to know what is ultimately motivating our communication with them. The only way they can truly know our intention is if we pay the price of revealing our heart....

The most dramatic example of an open heart speaking is one that changed the course of history and continues to redirect countless lives today: "The Word became flesh and made his dwelling among us. We have seen his glory, the glory of the One and Only, who came from the Father, full of grace and truth" (John 1:14). Jesus communicated with us by leaving His home in heaven, coming to this earth, and putting on human flesh so He could reveal His heart to us. ~

8. What about Jesus' heart is most compelling to you?

Break Through the Static

↳ [God] wants you to call on Him so He can help connect you with the people in your life. He will open up their hearts. That's how Christ communicated with us, by connecting with His Father. I communicate so much better with the people in my life when I connect with my heavenly Father first....

God tells us, "Call to me and I will answer you and tell you great and unsearchable things you do not know" (Jeremiah 33:3). When we call on Him, we never get a busy signal. He never puts us on hold. When we don't have the words to convey how we feel, when we have hard things to share that will hurt those we love, when we need to find the time and place to tell people how much they mean to us, we can ask Him for help. Be honest about it and ask, "God, give me the words to say to my wife to really show her how much I love her." "Lord, give me the words to say to my teenagers to really break through to them because it's hard right now." "Heavenly Father, help me know what to say to the friend I've lied to."...

All we have to do is ask. "But if any of you lacks wisdom, let him ask of God, who gives to all generously" (James 1:5, NASB). ↳

9. Take a few minutes to pray and ask God this question: "Whom do You want me to communicate and connect with today? What do You want me to tell them?" Thank God in advance for helping you make this connection!

Journal Your Life

Based on your study of this session of the guide, record your thoughts related to loving completely. Who needs more of the love you have to give?

_____

_____

_____

_____

_____

_____

_____

_____

_____

Small Group Discussion

Before you begin, take turns sharing any exciting and insightful experiences related to the thirty-days-to-live experiment.

1. Why do you value close relationships?

2. What attitudes and actions make relationships strong?

3. What causes relationships to deteriorate?

4. Jesus said, "For if you forgive men when they sin against you, your heavenly Father will also forgive you. But if you do not forgive men their sins, your Father will not forgive your sins" (Matthew 6:14–15). Why do you think forgiveness is so important to God? What happens to a person who does not forgive?

5. Take turns sharing stories about the power of forgiveness *and* unforgiveness.

6. Inevitably, there is friction in relationships. In your experience, what are the primary causes of such conflict?

7. What helps you reduce friction in your relationships?

8. Jesus said that we should take the plank out of our own eye before trying to take the speck out of another person's eye. Why is that such great advice? If you wish, share a story from your life that illustrates the wisdom of this advice.

9. With what we've learned studying the material on "love completely," what changes do you plan to make in your relationships?

Conclude with prayer for one another.

Next Session: Learn Humbly

Before the next session:

- Review days 16–22 in the book *One Month to Live*.
- Read and answer the Engage, Explore, and Enact sections in session 4 of this guide.
- Visit www.OneMonthToLive.com to learn more about how to live your life to the fullest.

Bonus Small Group Discussion

If your group wants to spend more time (perhaps an additional session) exploring the topic of loving completely, here are some additional excerpts from *One Month to Live* as well as questions for personal meditation and group discussion.

Fight Fair to Whip Conflict

None of us will love others well for very long if we don't know how to handle the disagreements that are as predictable as the sunrise. Fights happen: fighting fair has to be learned.

    ➣ I recently visited Lee Canalito's Boxing Gym in downtown Houston, where I worked with Ray Sugaroso to learn how to box. His goal was to train me to go a few rounds with some of the gym's best fighters. My goal was to avoid permanent damage to my middle-aged body!

    I survived but gained a whole new respect for boxers. Even though my opponents took it easy on me, one landed a blow to my chin that gave me a headache for the rest of the week....

Just as I had no idea how to box, most of us have no idea how to resolve conflict. Conflict is inevitable in relationships; when two unique and imperfect people come together, they simply won't agree about everything. That's why it's critical that we learn how to deal effectively with relationship issues. No one really teaches us how to confront and resolve the impasses that life inevitably brings, especially in marriage. ✒

1. How did your parents teach you to resolve conflict? Why was their instruction effective or not effective?

✒ The Bible provides us with principles for a fair fight....

One guideline that sounds simple can be the most difficult to maintain: stay in the ring and off the ropes....

We've all devised conflict-management tactics that reflect our temperaments, our experiences, or the examples we had growing up. Most of us have embraced one of five primary styles of fighting.

The first is what I call the rope-a-dope fighter, a style invented by Muhammad Ali in his prime. In the heat of the fight, he would lean into and bounce against the ropes, covering himself up and no longer swinging a punch....

Rope-a-dope fighters are "no way" resolvers, people who say, "There's no way you're getting me into a fight." They avoid conflict, refuse to engage, and retreat when emotions arise. Their number one rule is avoid conflict at all costs....

Next is the knockout artist, the one whose fighting stance is "It's my way or the highway." These relational boxers fight until they win and the other person gives in....

Then there's the take-the-fall fighter. These fighters throw in the towel early. They're always the first to give in. They become doormats, martyrs, as they roll over and play dead....

Fourth, the one-two puncher is committed to a give-and-take resolution. You win half, and I'll win half. I give in sometimes; you give in sometimes....

However, the best style is the sparring partner, the person committed to being a teammate and helping their partner. Sparring partners stay in the ring and off the ropes. Regardless of how unpleasant it becomes, they stay at it until they come to a mutual decision that they feel is best for both. Sparring partners realize the relationship is more important than anything they could argue about, and they understand that the process is usually more vital than the outcome. ❧

2. Which of these fighting "styles" matches your approach to resolving conflict?

3. The apostle James wrote, "What causes fights and quarrels among you? Don't they come from your desires that battle within you? You want something but don't get it. You kill and covet, but you cannot have what you want. You quarrel and fight. You do not have, because you do not ask God. When you ask, you do not receive, because you ask with wrong motives, that you may spend what you get on your pleasures" (4:1–3). Have you seen this progression in conflict?

4. How can we deal with our anger so that fighting fair is even possible?

5. What are some practical things two people in conflict can do to make them sparring partners instead of opponents?

～ The most important thing you can do is to bring the Prince of Peace into the ring with you. It takes three to build a great marriage: a husband, a wife, and God. You don't just bring Him into your corner and say, "God, help me win this argument." No, you invite Him into the whole situation because He's the only one who can meet your deepest needs. ～

6. Why will we fight more fairly if Jesus is in the ring?

7. If you only had a month to live, how might you handle conflict differently?

Learn Humbly

Related background reading for this session: Days 16–22 in One Month to Live.

If we only had one month to live, wouldn't we want to know that our lives were perfectly aligned with God's plans for us? Maybe even more so, at any point in our journey, it's nice to know who we are and where we are headed. To find such answers requires a humble, teachable heart.

Engage

⌒ I love to stargaze, to look up into the sky on a clear summer night and see hundreds, maybe thousands, of glittering jewels pierce the darkness. During these moments I'm reminded of how small I am and of how large God is.…

In one of his poems that we know as the psalms, David reveals that he had the same question. "When I look up into the night skies and see the work of your fingers—the moon and the stars you have made—I cannot understand how you can bother with mere puny man, to pay any attention to him!

And yet you have made him only a little lower than the angels" (Psalm 8:3–5, TLB)....

The answer to David's question is the same as God's response to us. God repeatedly and emphatically tells us, "You mean so much to me. I have a grand purpose for your life."...

So how do we discover who we were meant to be?... First, you have to look up to the Source of your creation if you're truly going to comprehend who you are and what you were created to do. ❧

1. What does it mean to you to be created in God's image, just a "little lower than the angels"?

❧ When I look at creation, I see a Creator, and I also see what kind of Creator He is. I see His personality, His power, and His playfulness. I see how much He loves uniqueness and variety. Think about the duckbill platypus or a monarch butterfly. Or consider your own body. If you don't believe that God loves variety, just go to the nearest mall, sit on one of the benches, and watch the wonderfully diverse people walking by...

[The apostle Paul wrote,] "For we are God's workmanship, created in Christ Jesus to do good works, which God prepared in advance for us to do" (Ephesians 2:10). ❧

2. What do you think Paul meant by "good works" in this verse?

3. Do you have a clear idea—or not—of the works God has prepared for you?

Warning: Watch for Identity Theft

🙠 Identify theft is not a new phenomenon—in fact, it's one of the oldest in the book, our Enemy's number one strategy. He wants to steal your awareness of who you really are. While God's purpose is to bring you life to the fullest, Satan has a plan for you to settle for so much less than what you were made for. The thief's plan is to steal, kill, and destroy. He knows if he can steal your identity, he will destroy your dreams and your purpose in life. You and I need to constantly be aware that we are at the center of an epic battle. 🙠

4. How would you describe your identity in Christ?

5. How has Satan attempted to steal your identity?

Explore

‧ GPS isn't just for navigating between geographic locations. It represents a great way to consider what God has instilled in us to help us find the road to an abundant life....

We must be willing to activate the GPS that our Creator has installed in us. If we're going to find our way through the many circumstances and choices of life, we must be willing to use three crucial resources: our **Gifts**, our **Passions**, and our **Struggles**. ‧

Gifts

‧ How do you discover what God has given you? Ask yourself what you do well and answer honestly. Ask your Creator, the One who made you. And ask your friends and family, "What do you see as my main gifts, my primary strengths? Where do you see my talents most clearly on display?" ‧

1. Make a list of what you believe are God's gifts to you. Don't be shy—write everything down.

2. Which of these gifts are you using to advance God's kingdom?

Passions

❧ We find our place and purpose in life when we discover our passion. Paul wrote in Romans, "Never be lazy in your work, but serve the Lord enthusiastically" (12:11, NLT).... If my gifts are the engine I'm given, then my passion is the fuel that packs a punch and keeps me going....

So how do you discover what your true passion is? Ask Him. Pay attention to what you enjoy doing. Take note when you find yourself caught up in the joy of an experience, whether it's gardening or teaching, running or baking. When you enjoy doing something, the time flies and your emotions with it. It may be hard work, but your love of the thing transcends the sweat and effort. Living in the midst of what you're passionate about will also delight God....

God feels the same way about you. When you pursue the passions He has placed in your heart, He simply loves it. ❧

3. Where do you see passion in your life? What really floats your boat?

Struggles

❧ It makes sense that our gifts and passions help us find our way and fulfill the abundant lives God wants for us. However, the third force in our GPS— struggles—is every bit as important as the other two…. Why? Because when God allows us to go through struggles, problems, and difficulties, we learn to depend on Him….

Being the creative God that He is, our Father always uses our wounds to make us stronger and to help those around us. "He comes alongside us when we go through hard times, and before you know it, he brings us alongside someone else who is going through hard times so that we can be there for that person just as God was there for us" (2 Corinthians 1:4, MSG).

God allows problems and struggles into your life so you can come alongside others and help them….

By providing you a GPS system, God has equipped you to avoid the detours and dead ends of the conformity trap. You have creative license to be who God made you to be. The great theologian Dr. Seuss once said, "Be who you are because those who mind don't matter and those who matter don't mind." ❧

4. What struggles have you endured?

5. How has God used your pain to encourage and comfort others?

6. Whom might you come alongside now?

Surviving Hurricanes of Change

Like a mighty river, life has a current that never stands still. One of life's most important lessons is that change is a constant.

❤ The only permanent thing in life is change. The Bible reminds us, "To everything there is a season, a time for every purpose under heaven" (Ecclesiastes 3:1, NKJV). Change is just a part of life.

The winds of change will either make you stronger or knock you down. In marriage the problems and trials will either draw you closer together or destroy your relationship....

Human nature inclines us to look only at the immediate problem and its collateral damage rather than any potential positive outcomes....

God doesn't cause the painful changes in our lives, but He uses them and wants to bring good out of them....

As we've seen, the Bible addresses all aspects of what it means to be fully alive. Surviving the hurricane winds of change in life is no exception. By putting biblical principles into practice, we'll see that we can not only survive the winds of change, but we can harness them to fill our sails and propel us forward.…

The reality is that if we don't learn to adapt to the winds of change, we'll never enjoy life. Change is frightening, uncertain, and threatening, but it can also be healthy, dynamic, refreshing, and necessary. ◄

7. What are some of the significant changes you have experienced?

8. Which of these changes did you weather well? Which ones not so well? What made the difference?

◄ While we must learn to adapt and change course to ride out the storm, we also have to know when to drop anchor and stay fixed in place.… You need an anchor that never changes: "Jesus Christ is the same yesterday and today and forever" (Hebrews 13:8). While everything else is changing around you, God never changes. He's the same God as He was in Bible times. He can work the same miracles in your life today, and He'll be the same God tomorrow....

Too often we wait on someone or something external to change us. We blame our spouses for not fulfilling us emotionally, our churches or pastors for not fulfilling us spiritually, our jobs for not fulfilling our sense of purpose.... It's time to take responsibility for our own growth. ~

9. How do we take responsibility for our own growth?

10. What are some areas you would like to grow in?

Enact

Beyond the familiar disciplines of the Christian life—actions like prayer, study of the Word, sharing your faith, serving others—what are some less obvious factors that make a significant contribution to spiritual maturity?

Slow Down

⌒ Spiritual growth and transformation will never occur in your life until you finally get still, until you stop moving....

People who discover that their time is limited often make radical lifestyle changes. They give up workaholism and slow down the pace of their lives, spending time with loved ones, with God, and alone, reflecting on their lives. They relinquish the pursuit and collection of material possessions and finally enjoy the fullness of what they already have. They rediscover the simple pleasures of curling up by a fire with a good book or sharing a picnic in the shade of a huge oak tree on a summer day. Their physical condition may force them to slow down, but most welcome the opportunity to get off the hyperspeed treadmills that their lives had become. ⌒

1. Do you feel you are on a hyperspeed treadmill? If yes, how might you slow the treadmill down or even step off it?

⌒ Our restlessness manifests itself as a dis-ease of the soul, a growing discontent that has reached epic proportions in our twenty-first-century society. We make much more money and enjoy many more conveniences than our grandparents did, yet most of us are not happier....

The only place to remedy the restlessness in our soul is inside. In his letter to the Romans, Paul describes how we begin such a transformation: "Do not conform any longer to the pattern of this world, but be transformed by the renewing of your mind. Then you will be able to test and approve what God's will is—his good, pleasing and perfect will" (Romans 12:2).

In Paul's prescription here, the key word "transformed" comes from the Greek word *metamorphous,* from which we get *metamorphosis,* literally meaning "to be changed from the inside out." ❧

2. What patterns of the world do you *not* want to be conformed to?

3. Spiritual transformation is often preceded by loss. That is tough, but how can we learn how to be good "losers"?

❧ One of the most difficult lessons in life is how to accept loss. And it's an ongoing process since our lives constantly change and we're forced to confront the harsh realities of a world that's far from perfect. Whether you are single or married, a teacher or a student, a business executive or a stay-at-home mom, you have most likely faced some moment when your world was shaken to its foundation....

During these times, our faith can be shaken to the core. On one hand, such trials and painful losses force us to depend on God—for comfort, for peace, for His love and mercy. But on the other, we may become angry and resistant to Him because we can't imagine why He would allow such a tragedy, loss, or catastrophe in the first place.... But God never abandons us. He suffers right along with us.... In fact, look at what Jesus says: "In this world you will have trouble. But take heart! I have overcome the world" (John 16:33)....

When the earthquakes of life hit, we find out what we're made of and what we've structured our lives upon....

An unshakable foundation is also the key to building a meaningful life.... Jesus uses this common-sense truth to illustrate our need for a supernatural foundation that can withstand any disaster or tragedy we encounter: "Everyone who hears these words of mine and puts them into practice is like a wise man who built his house on the rock. The rain came down, the streams rose, and the winds blew and beat against that house; yet it did not fall, because it had its foundation on the rock" (Matthew 7:24–25). ⋙

4. How has God been a rock in your life?

Ask for Peace

⋙ God wants you to turn to Him first when trouble hits. But we try to solve all our problems, and then, as a last resort, as our lives begin to crumble around us and our resources are exhausted, we finally turn to God and say, "Well, I guess there's nothing left to do but pray!"...

This formula is backward; prayer should be our first response, not our last resort. God says, "Turn to Me first, pray about it, because I'm right here with you." How do you know if God is truly the center of your life? You stop worrying! Whenever you start worrying about something, it's a signal that God's been pushed out of first place, and something else has supplanted Him as the center of your life. Whenever you put God first in an area, you stop worrying about it. If God's not first in your marriage, you worry about your relationship. If He's not first in your finances, you fret over your bank account. If God's not first in your business, you can't sleep at night for thinking about the office. Whenever we begin to worry, we've lost our shelter and exposed ourselves to the elements that can shake our faith. ~

5. What are your worries now? List them here. Then, in prayer, turn them over to God. Thank Him for His concern and, in advance, for His answers!

Depend on Your Team

~ Another primary practice for securing your foundation is having a community that cares, a human support system. You need a team of people around you who love you for who you are and not for what you do. You need some friends in your life who will walk in when everyone else walks out....

God designed a way to meet this need we all have for community: the church. When one person or family experiences an earthquake, the rest of us gather around and help them remain strong, assist them in rebuilding, and take care of them. ⤳

6. How has the church encouraged you in times of trouble?

7. Whom do you know in your faith community who could use your love and care?

A Whole Life

⤳ [Integrity.] This word gets used a lot today, especially in political circles, but what does it really mean? The root of the word *integrity* is "integer." As you'll recall from math class, an integer is simply a whole number as opposed to a fraction. So integrity means wholeness as opposed to being fragmented and fractured in life. When you lack integrity, you end up acting one way at church and another way at work or at school. You act one way with your friends and another way at home with your family…. "Better to be a poor person who has integrity than to be rich and double-dealing" (Proverbs 28:6, God's Word). ❧

8. As you complete this session, ask God to reveal any areas of your life that could use more integrity. You are not alone; we all have such areas. Thank God for His ongoing support in helping you "learn humbly" what He wants for your life.

Journal Your Life

Based on your study of this session of the guide, record your thoughts related to learning humbly. How do you think God wants you to grow in this season of life?

_____

_____

_____

_____

_____

_____

_____

_____

_____

_____

_____

_____

_____

_____

_____

_____

Small Group Discussion

Take a few minutes to review the journey of each group member since you were last together.

1. What are some of the ways we can learn how to live the lives God intends for us?

2. What role does humility play in such learning?

3. In *One Month to Live* we read, "If you only had one month to live, you would want to stop the ceaseless motion of a busy life and find ways to enjoy stillness and solitude." Share experiences of how getting alone with God resulted in learning and growth in your spiritual life.

4. "When we get real with God and others, when we're being who God created us to be rather than trying to pretend we're someone else, then our distinct individual beauty emerges" (from *One Month to Live*). Do you find it difficult to relax and be you? Why or why not?

5. A symptom of soul disease is comparison compulsion—always having to be sure we know who we are and what we're worth. Why are we so driven to look to others for approval and a sense of identity?

6. What was Christ's response to the peer pressure He faced?

7. "Donald O. Clifton, in his book *Living Your Strengths,* says from a very young age we are taught to be 'well rounded.'… It's an insult to God when we focus on the gifts and passions we don't have and try to develop only our weak areas. Our greatest potential lies in the areas of our greatest strengths" (from *One Month to Live)*. Do you agree or disagree with this idea—that we should concentrate on our strengths rather than trying to build up our weaknesses? Why do you feel this way?

8. "Alfred Souza observed, 'For a long time it had seemed to me that life was about to begin—real life. But there was always some obstacle in the way,

something to be gotten through first, some unfinished business, time to still be served, a debt to be paid. Then life would begin. At last it dawned on me that these obstacles were my life'" (from *One Month to Live*). Can you relate to what Souza said? Do you welcome obstacles and problems as ways to grow, or do you try to avoid them as much as possible?

9. Life always involves problems, pain, and loss. Some people thrive in adversity while others wither. What makes the difference?

10. Our problems often are the result of Satan's efforts to destroy us. "As C. S. Lewis put it, 'There is no neutral ground in the universe; every square inch, every split second is claimed by God and counterclaimed by Satan'" (from *One Month to Live*). What evidence do you see of the larger spiritual conflict of which your life is a part?

Wrap up with prayer for one another.

Next Session: Leave Boldly

Before the next session:

- Review days 23–28 in the book *One Month to Live*.
- Read and answer the Engage, Explore, and Enact sections in session 5 of this guide.
- Visit www.OneMonthToLive.com to learn more about how to live your life to the fullest.

Bonus Small Group Discussion

If your group wants to spend more time (perhaps an additional session) exploring the topic of learning humbly, here are some additional excerpts from *One Month to Live* as well as questions for personal meditation and group discussion.

Seeking a Miracle

Do you believe that God is in the miracle business?

➜ If you only had one month to live, the temptation might be to plead with God for a miracle to extend your life. And while our lives are clearly in His hands, and He can definitely heal physically, the miracle you truly need might have more to do with your priorities and relationships. ➜

1. Have you experienced a miracle or do you know someone who has? Share your stories with others in the group.

➜ Miracles are not only possible; they're more common than we think. God cares for us and wants to work in our lives. The hard part is remembering this when we come to a crossroads and must choose how to respond.... Whether we're facing a painful loss or confronted with choosing between two good options, the only way to experience the miraculous is to move in God's direction. There's definitely no formula, but in the Bible I find four road signs that can help us transform those forks in the road into a fulfilling, miraculous journey. ∽

In the Old Testament book of 2 Kings we see the story of the prophet Elisha and the widow. This impoverished lady had not only lost her husband, but a creditor was threatening to claim her two sons as slaves (definitely a different time!). Elisha asked the woman what she had in her house. She remembered she had only "a little oil" and that was all that was needed for a miracle!

∽ Here we see the process God always uses when He wants to work a miracle in our lives. It begins with a dire situation and a plea for help....

If you want God to work a miracle in your life, you have to realize there are two one-way streets you have to travel on to start the miracle. The first one is to admit your need....

The first one-way street—admitting your need—leads to the second one-way street—going to God as the only One who can lead you in the right direction. Where do you go when you have a problem? Do you call the psychic hotline or consult your horoscope? People try all kinds of things when they are in need, and it seems the more desperate we become, the crazier we get in looking to outside sources for help. There's only one outside source who can provide the miracles we need. We can go directly to God, the only One with the power, wisdom, and love to focus on our best interests. ∽

2. How hard is it for you to admit you need help?

3. Be honest. Do you ever seek help first from sources other than God when you are in a jam? What are these other sources?

    ⚫ Now we're prepared for the next road sign on our journey—a stop sign.... Like the needy widow, we often get so caught up in what we don't have that we overlook the possibilities of what He's already given us.

    God had already given this woman the beginnings of her miracle; she just didn't recognize it. We have to stop and assess what we have to work with.... God asks, "Well, what do I have to work with? Stop worrying and start looking!" So you have to take everything you have and give it to Him. Your time, talent, resources, and energy, no matter how limited they may seem, are God's starting place. Your willingness and surrender activate God's intervention and blessings. ⚫

4. As you think of challenges you're facing now, what has God already given you "to work with"?

⌐ If you're going to see God transform your circumstances into His destiny for your life, you need to follow the third road sign and make a U-turn from a negative direction to a positive. Our first reaction when problems come our way tends to be negative. With sweeping exaggerations, we declare that everything is bad, nothing is good, and there's no hope.…

This shift in direction requires faith.… Faith is not ignoring the present reality; it's acknowledging that with God all things are possible. It's not faith to pretend that a problem doesn't exist—that's either stupidity or denial. Faith doesn't deny the problem; it helps you see it from a new perspective, through God's eyes.…

God loves to take the little bit we have and multiply it, because then He alone gets the credit. ⌐

5. Why would pretending a problem doesn't exist not be an example of faith?

6. Share some examples of how God has used "the little" in your life to accomplish great results.

The fourth sign on the road to a miracle is the most important one: the yield sign. If you follow the other three signs but don't follow this one, you can't expect a miracle. It's essential that we begin serving others with the blessings He's already given us....

This is just the opposite of my natural reaction to need. When I have a problem, my attitude becomes "I can't focus on anyone else's needs right now; I have needs of my own. I don't have time for anyone else; I'm overwhelmed and need to take care of myself first." My first inclination is to hoard the little bit of time, resources, and energy that I have.

7. Why is it important to give ourselves to others?

It's a paradox that we may never fully understand. When we move the focus off ourselves and onto God and start pouring our life into others and yielding to His direction, then He starts pouring His miracles into us. As counterintuitive as it may seem, the best advice I can give you when you're going through a problem is to look for empty vessels to pour yourself into.

8. What are some empty vessels that you can pour yourself into now?

Leave Boldly

Related background reading for this session: Days 23–28 in One Month to Live.

Individuals in public life, such as American presidents, often seem driven to ask, "How will history judge me and my administration?" Often in the last years of a second term, a president will seek to secure his legacy.

There certainly is nothing wrong with asking how we will be remembered. But the ultimate quest for a follower of Jesus is to finish the trek here on earth and hear from the Lord Himself the words, "Well done, good and faithful servant."

That's the bold finish—the legacy—I long for.

Engage

～ I love watching my kids make sandcastles whenever we go to the beach. Now that they're older, it doesn't happen as often, but they used to sit for hours, digging and smoothing, shoveling and patting, trying to get the turrets just right.... I remember when they were really small how shocked they would always be as the tide started to roll in. The waves would creep higher and higher until the foam began to lick the edges of their castle, and finally it was washed away....

Unfortunately, I've witnessed too many people at the end of their lives feeling the same way. They work nonstop, ever busy with a hectic, over-booked schedule. Then eventually their bodies force them to slow down and take a look at what they've struggled so hard to construct. The harsh reality they often face is that much of what they strove for won't last. After they die, it will wash away like a sandcastle at high tide. ↩

1. What kinds of things do people work so hard to acquire or achieve that will wash away quickly when their lives on earth end?

↩ As we...focus on the principle of leaving boldly, it is so important to understand the investment required to leave a lasting legacy before it's too late. If you only had one month to live, you could make some changes that would improve what you left behind. But how much better to know that you're contributing to your legacy every day over many months and years and that all you're working for will last for eternity. ↩

2. What will last for eternity?

3. Of those things, what will mean the most to you?

Explore

❧ If we're going to leave a legacy that the waves of time can't wash away, we need to do an on-site inspection of the life we're currently building....

God has invested in each of us the ability to influence others, and He expects a return on His investment. He wants us to take advantage of our opportunities rather than burying our heads in the sand and ignoring our responsibility to make a difference in the lives of others....

My life, my time, is not my own. It belongs to Christ, and it's His name that will last; only when I live to influence others for Him will I leave an enduring legacy. You and I will be forgotten one day. Only what we do for God, how we fulfill the purpose for which He made us, will remain. ❧

1. Take a personal inventory: List the names of the people in your life whom you influence in more than a casual way.

2. What surprises you about this list? What kind of a "return on investment" is God getting from your life, as it relates to the people you influence?

Passing the Affluence Test

If you're going to have an impact on eternity, you have to consider how you spend your material resources. You may be tempted to think, *Wait a minute, I'm barely getting by. I'm certainly not affluent! This must apply only to wealthy folks.* I understand where you're coming from, but with very few exceptions, if you're reading this book, you're considered affluent by the rest of the world. Passing the affluence inspection is not as dependent on the amount of money you have as what you do with it....

There's nothing wrong with having resources and wealth as long as we realize that all the material things we have are just sandcastles....

The only way to pass the affluence test is by giving. We must learn to be givers rather than takers so we can make a difference.

3. Do you consider yourself rich? Why or why not?

4. If you had just thirty days to live, would you be more generous with your resources or not? Explain your reasoning.

Lasting Treasure

⟿ When you use your influence and affluence to obey God, He will enable you to leave behind a permanent inheritance....

Paul wrote in Ephesians 5:15–17, "So be careful how you live, not as fools but as those who are wise. Make the most of every opportunity for doing good in these evil days. Don't act thoughtlessly, but try to understand what the Lord wants you to do" (NLT). This may be the greatest secret to leaving a legacy of substance: try to understand what the Lord wants you to do—and do it. Obey God, because He gives you just enough time to do everything you need to do, both in your day and in your life....

Obedience always leads to God's blessing. ⟿

5. What do you think God wants you to do with your life? If you have not considered this question carefully, do so prayerfully in the coming days.

⮞ As we think about what it means to make decisions as if we only had one month to live, the question remains: Is it possible to live in such a way that the impact of our lives is felt forever? I not only believe it's possible; I believe it's the kind of life we were made for. The Psalmist reveals how to live a life that outlasts you: "Generation after generation stands in awe of your work; each one tells stories of your mighty acts" (Psalm 145:4, MSG)....

Bottom line, it all comes down to the power of the seed.

In Matthew chapter 13, we find Jesus telling the parable of the sower: "A farmer went out to sow his seed. As he was scattering the seed, some fell along the path, and the birds came and ate it up. Some fell on rocky places, where it did not have much soil. It sprang up quickly, because the soil was shallow. But when the sun came up, the plants were scorched, and they withered because they had no root. Other seed fell among thorns, which grew up and choked the plants. Still other seed fell on good soil, where it produced a crop—a hundred, sixty or thirty times what was sown" (verses 3–8).

At its most basic level, this is a parable about faith because the farmer has faith in the seed, in its ability to yield a crop. In essence he's planting a seed of faith. ⮞

6. What "seeds of faith" has God prompted you to sow in your life? (dreams? passions? goals? opportunities? open doors?)

7. What sacrifices might be required of you to see these seeds sprout, grow, and bear a huge crop?

     ✎ Every day, every moment, with every action, you're planting something. So the question is, what exactly are you planting?.... Unfortunately, some of us spend our time planting rocks—no potential, no life, no fruit....

     The crucial test in determining if we're planting real seeds or just rocks emerges in our motivation for planting. Am I sowing seed to meet my own needs or to meet the needs of others? ✎

8. What are some effective ways to continually evaluate our motives?

⟋ In John 12:24, Jesus explains, "I tell you the truth, unless a kernel of wheat falls to the ground and dies, it remains only a single seed. But if it dies, it produces many seeds." The seed has to go into the ground, and in the silence of the ground, it dies. All alone there, it opens up to bring forth life.... If we invest in people's lives, then our legacy becomes like a giant oak, providing life for generations to come....

If you plant temporary things, you are going to harvest temporary things. If you plant eternal seeds, you are going to harvest eternal fruit. If you plant generosity, you are going to harvest generosity. If you give grace and compassion, you are going to get grace and compassion. Whatever you give out in life, you are going to get back. According to the law of the harvest, we reap *what* we sow, but we also reap much *more* than we sow. If I plant one seed, I don't get one seed or even one apple in return but a tree full of apples, season after season. A bushel of blessing comes from a tiny seed of faith. ⟋

9. Have you experienced the "law of the harvest" in your life? Share some examples with the group.

Build for Eternity

⟋ One of our core desires is to leave this earth a better place than when we entered it. We're designed by our Creator to fulfill a vital purpose that no one else can accomplish but us. We're hard-wired with the longing to have an impact, to make a difference that will echo throughout eternity long after our bodies have turned to dust....

Our legacy is determined by how we spend our days. ❧

10. How does the thought of leaving a legacy influence your daily life?

❧ If you want to ensure a legacy that will outlast you,...you need three key building materials.

The first one is your convictions—what you stand for. Convictions are those core values from God's Word that never change; they're eternal. Trends and styles—they come and go, "but the word of our God stands forever" (Isaiah 40:8)....

The next eternal building material emerges in our character. When we die, we don't take anything with us except our character, who we are at our core....

There are several methods God uses to cultivate Christ's character in us. The first comes with the problems of life. As difficult as they are, problems always have a purpose. Sometimes God allows distractions in your life, those little irritations that rub off the rough edges of your character. Other times He gets out the jackhammer and starts chipping away those huge chunks that don't look like Jesus. If we embrace the problems of life as opportunities to trust Him and become more like Christ, then we don't have nearly as much room to worry, feel sorry for ourselves, or get angry.

God also uses the pressures of life to smooth our edges....

Finally, He likes to use the people in our lives to enrich our character, to chip away at our selfish edges that prevent us from loving others the way Christ does.

[The third key building material] is community. Godly convictions and godly character last forever, and our relationships with God's people last forever as well. If we are to forge a bridge that leads to an eternal destination, then we need teammates—people committed to the same passion for God and His Word....

If you're too busy to commit to ongoing time with a group of like-minded individuals, then you're just too busy. ⌒

11. Take a few minutes to write down the bedrock values that you base your life on. For each value on your list, ask yourself, "Does this value come from God's Word or from somewhere else?"

12. When you leave this earth, what character qualities do you want to take with you?

13. What are your ongoing meaningful connections to the body of Christ? Are these connections adequate, or do they need some improvement?

⟨ Most of the material possessions we'll leave behind won't last much longer than we did.... I recently saw an antique store called Dead People's Stuff. That's funny, but it's an honest description of what all our possessions will someday be. But if we build our lives on convictions, character, and community, then we will have established an eternal memorial that will benefit countless lives for untold generations. ⟩

Enact

Do you believe that your life could change the world? Most of us don't feel we have that kind of power or influence. But how do we know the potential impact of our role in God's great plan? He is such a Master of detail that we can be confident He is using every moment of our lives to advance His objectives. That's why every day counts—whether we have thirty days or thirty years left on earth.

⟨ If you discovered that you only had one month to live and you began considering how you could leave a lasting global legacy, you might be tempted to think, *It's too late. I don't have the money or power needed to make a difference in this world.* But never underestimate the power of *one.* It's the ability each of us has, every day, to be used by God to bless the rest of the world....

When we are reminded on the nightly newscast of global problems like world hunger, the AIDS epidemic, war, and famine, we often respond with numbing apathy or resigned defeat. Most of us are tempted to think, *Why even try? The issue is so enormous and complex that I'll never make a difference.* There is a temptation to make these problems abstractions instead of daily realities for individual human lives.… If we touch one life, we may make the difference between life and death—physical as well as spiritual—for another human being. If we make it a habit to do what we can, when we can, where we can, we will be transformed as we help others.

1. How has your life been influenced positively by others? Make a list of several people who have encouraged you during your journey and modeled admirable qualities. Beside the name of each person, describe how that person influenced you.

2. Make another list. This time record the names of people you have the opportunity to serve through modeling a godly life. Beside each name write some ideas of how you can be more proactive and effective in your modeling and encouragement.

Heart for the World

↩ We rarely face it, but many of us have a nagging question in the depths of our soul. How do we reconcile the fact that we're living in nice homes, driving nice cars, and eating plenty of food while most of the world lives on less than two dollars a day?…

I'm not trying to make you feel guilty, only to remind you that we have lost our perspective. We've lost our ability to see beyond our own lives for two primary reasons. One is the human desire to control our own safe and comfortable world. The other is that our culture drives us to acquire more rather than give away more.

If we knew our time on earth was running out, we'd want to do all we could to impact others. We wouldn't want the regret of a life misspent and self-absorbed. We would want to know that we honored the God we love by being the very best stewards of all He has given us. In his letter to the Romans, Paul wrote, "Therefore, I urge you, brothers, in view of God's mercy, to offer your bodies as living sacrifices, holy and pleasing to God—this is your spiritual act of worship. Do not conform any longer to the pattern of this world, but be transformed by the renewing of your mind. Then you will be able to test and approve what God's will is—his good, pleasing and perfect will" (12:1–2).…

Paul reveals the secret to maturity: we must move from our focus on self-comfort and become living sacrifices. The goal of maturity is to move beyond ourselves and our own desires. If we truly want to grow in our character and our faith, then we must be willing to change our goal from one of safety to one of sacrifice. ↩

3. In your experience, what do you depend upon to feel safe and secure?

4. What are some areas of your life where you would like, as an act of worship, to offer yourself more as a living sacrifice?

⌒ One of the first and most important ways we can begin to care more about others is to pray for the poor and oppressed throughout the world. Pray for their needs. For their healing. For religious and political freedom. For food and clean water and vital medicine….

God says it's okay to be blessed financially as long as we do two things with our money and possessions. Number one: enjoy what we have instead of always wanting more. And number two: give generously. ⌒

Go for It!

⌒ If you want to experience the full adventure that your life is intended to be, then you have to be willing to take action and serve those in need with

God's love. The Bible has a lot to say about caring for the needs of the poor. "If a man shuts his ears to the cry of the poor, he too will cry out and not be answered" (Proverbs 21:13). God holds us accountable for how we use our blessings to help the poor and hurting.

Our greatest gifts—time, talents, and treasures—are essential to this process of maturing and building a global legacy....

But think about what you can do. Consider the expertise you have in the jobs you've worked—whether it's construction, banking, sales, medicine, or education. You have knowledge, abilities, and skills that can change the lives of others if you'll only share them. Can you listen and care? offer a smile? hug a child? Most of us underestimate the power we have just by being present in the life of someone else....

The final way we grow in maturity and create a world-conscious heart is to work in community. Whether it's through our churches, our schools, our companies, our neighborhoods, or our families, we're called to come together to help others.

5. What abilities do you have that could be shared to improve the lives of others?

Journal Your Life

Based on your study of this session of the guide, record your thoughts related to leaving boldly. What do you want to be remembered for?

_____

_____

_____

_____

_____

_____

_____

_____

_____

Small Group Discussion

Take some time to compare notes on the thirty-day challenge. With this experiment nearly done, encourage one another to press on and gain the benefits of a careful analysis of your lives.

1. What are some sandcastles you have built in your life that later washed away? What did you learn in the process?
2. How often do you think about your legacy?
3. Why are we prone to ignore the "bigger picture" of legacy and eternity?
4. The Bible uses "seed" as a metaphor for our attitudes and actions. What are examples of bad seed? examples of good seed?
5. Jesus once told a parable about the importance of the soil. As you look at your life, what are examples of good and bad soil, the environments where truth and godliness will flourish or wither?
6. This statement is in the book *One Month to Live:* "What we perceive as schedule-related collisions are usually values-based crashes. Our actions reveal a different set of values than what we say matters most to us." Do you agree or disagree with this assertion—that busyness and schedule conflicts have more to do with our values than with time management? Discuss your reasoning.
7. "As Ralph Waldo Emerson observed, 'There is no beautifier of complexion, or form, or behavior, like the wish to scatter joy and not pain around us'" (from *One Month to Live*). Why does serving others bring such joy?
8. The world has huge problems. What issues grip you the most?
9. How does God want us to view and respond to the big problems of the world such as disease, hunger, poverty, and illiteracy?
10. How do you think social action and spiritual outreach relate?

Close in prayer.

Next Session: Living Like There's No Tomorrow

Before the next session:

- Review days 29–30 in the book *One Month to Live*.
- Read and answer the Engage, Explore, and Enact sections in session 6 of this guide.
- Visit www.OneMonthToLive.com to learn more about how to live your life to the fullest.

Bonus Small Group Discussion

If your group wants to spend more time (perhaps an additional session) exploring the topic of leaving boldly, here are some additional excerpts from *One Month to Live* as well as questions for personal meditation and group discussion.

Living in God's Will

Living life to the fullest inevitably requires that we both know God and understand what He wants us to do.

    How do we stay in the middle of God's will? The Psalmist instructs us: "Trust in the LORD and do good; dwell in the land and enjoy safe pasture. Delight yourself in the LORD and he will give you the desires of your heart. Commit your way to the LORD; trust in him and he will do this" (Psalm 37:3–5).

    How do we avoid those nasty collisions where our will gets in the way of His perfect plan for our lives? If we break down this passage and dig deep, we're going to find three principles for staying in God's will. The first one is really an issue of trust: "Trust in the LORD and do good." If we trust God, then we'll want to obey Him rather than follow our own desires. If we don't trust Him, we'll want to get behind the steering wheel and take control....

[I have found that] it's really not so much about God's will as it is about God's wheel. It's really a struggle over control of the steering wheel.

We're always trying to wrestle the steering wheel away from God. We think we can drive better than He does. We're always telling Him how to drive and where to go, thinking, *I know what's best for my life.* 〜

1. In your experience, what questions or confusion have you had about God's will for your life?

2. In what areas of your life is it easier to trust God?

3. In what areas of your life is it harder to trust God?

☙ There is another principle to staying in God's will. Not only do I need to trust, but I also need to delight. The Psalmist says, "Delight yourself in the LORD and he will give you the desires of your heart" ([37:]4). This word "delight" in Hebrew means "to enjoy." When you delight in someone, you enjoy their company, and you want to spend time with them. We all want to receive the fulfillment of our heart's desires, and this scripture makes it clear that this is possible. But there's a condition—it's a promise with a premise. We must delight ourselves in the Lord *more* than we long for our heart's desires. ☙

4. Take turns sharing what "delighting in God" looks like in your own life. There are no exact right answers to this question, so be candid about your experiences of enjoying God.

☙ This is where many people seem to lose sight of what God's will is all about. We think He should let us drive the car if He really loves us. But He wants us to long to be with Him, to know Him, to love Him more than any destination we could ever reach on our own.

When our oldest son first got his driver's license, he couldn't wait to get out of the house and be independent. There was always a ball game, a study session, an event—something that required him to drive somewhere. But then one Friday night I was surprised to see him sitting at the dinner table with the rest of the family. I commented, "I'm glad to see you, but what are you doing here?" He smiled and quietly said, "I just wanted to hang at home tonight. Missed you guys." Wow. That made my day! God is the same way. He longs for us to delight in Him more than we delight in our own freedom. In fact, when we delight in Him, our heart's desires often change. We no longer want our way; we want His way. ❧

5. Why do we think that God is more interested in our being than our doing?

6. Can you recall some examples of letting go of your plan, following God, and *then* receiving something you deeply desired?

❧ Finally, if we're going to remain in the center of God's will, we must…
commit: "Commit your way to the LORD; trust in him and he will do this"

([Psalm 37:]5). We have to come to the place where we commit to following God's will. Often we say, "God, show me Your will, and I'll consider it as an option in this decision I'm making." God says, "No, you have to commit to following My will, and *then* I'll show you what it is." ☜

7. Why is our loyalty and commitment to Him so important to God?

☜ Maybe you feel like your life has crashed and the pieces are crumpled beyond recognition or repair. It seems you're the object of a lot of rubber-necking—a messed-up life that others stare at. I have news for you. It's not too late to change the course of your life! God still has a great plan for you, but the first step is to slide out of the driver's seat and ask God to take the wheel. Start giving Him the first consideration in every decision, and watch your life be transformed.

Which brings us back to trust. Obedience starts with trust and ends with trust. We step out in faith and allow God to drive our car and take us where He wants us to be. But it's not a passive process. He wants us to pay attention and take action along the way. ☜

8. If you are comfortable doing this, share one key area of your life where you want to trust God more. After group members have listed these, take turns

praying for one another. Ask for God's help in surrendering control and trusting Him in these critical areas of each person's life.

✎ Most of an enduring legacy results from actions we take in our lifetime. We say we want to be close to our loved ones, but this can only be accomplished through quality and quantity time, honest conversations, and shared sorrows and celebrations. We say we want to make a difference in this world, to leave it a better place than we found it. But we must take action, directed by our Father, to reach out to others, loving them, mentoring them, serving them. ✎

9. What is God saying to you now? Where do you think He wants you to start taking action in loving others?

✎ Our time in this life is limited. If we truly want to ensure that we've fulfilled our purpose when it's our time to go, then we must stay squarely in God's will, trusting, delighting, and committing to His path. He's the only One who can rebuild our lives and redirect us when our will collides with His. ✎

6

Living Like There's No Tomorrow

Related background reading for this session: Days 29–30 in One Month to Live.

What a great roller-coaster ride this has been! I trust by now you are seeing the benefits of living a more vital and intentional life. In this session we want to review several crucial concepts and offer insights that will spur you to even greater fulfillment beyond the thirty-day challenge.

How can we live like there's no tomorrow?

Engage

↝ When it comes to the game of life,…there will come a moment when the final buzzer sounds, and it's game over. In fact, statistics show that the human death rate is at a constant 100 percent! You can't avoid it; you can't cheat your way around it....

In Ecclesiastes, we're told, "A wise person thinks much about death, while the fool thinks only about having a good time now" (7:4, NLT)....

God put you on this earth for a reason, and He has a plan for your life. But this life is not the end. Scripture is very clear about this reality. One day you will stop breathing, but you won't stop living. You'll live forever in eternity.

One moment after you die, you'll experience either the greatest celebration ever or the greatest separation ever. Heaven and hell are real places, and we have the choice of where we will spend eternity. God could have created us as robots, programmed to love Him, serve Him, and follow Him. But He didn't do that. He took the greatest risk of all when He created us with this power called free will. God loves you so much that He died for you, but He lets you choose whether or not you will love Him back and desire to be with Him for all eternity....

Heaven is a perfect place for perfect people, and the problem is, we're not perfect. We've all sinned. That's why Christ came to take our place—so we could join Him in heaven one day. Not that we could ever deserve it, not that we could ever earn it, but He has made the way for us. The Bible says that, because of what Christ has done, we are friends with God. Right now you can pray and ask Christ to come into your life and forgive your past guilt and sins and give you a future in heaven one day. You don't have to be afraid of eternity. God loves you more than you can fathom. He truly does. You really can't make the most of every moment until you know your eternity is settled. That knowledge then frees you to enjoy life and to make a difference in others' lives.

1. When did you make a choice to confess your sins, believe in Christ, and ask Him into your life? If you're not sure you have ever made that decision, don't put it off—do it right now!

~ The Bible talks about heaven and uses human words to describe what is humanly indescribable. It says there will be streets of gold and gates of pearls. The place drips with value and significance, meaning and purpose. We'll have jobs there that will bring us ultimate fulfillment. Christ is there, so we will experience more compassion and creativity than we could ever dream of. We'll have new, perfect bodies. We'll be reunited with our family, friends, and loved ones who are there. ~

2. What excites you most about heaven?

3. Who are some of the people you've known whom you look forward to seeing in heaven?

Explore

❧ Once you're prepared for eternity, you want to invest in what will last forever as well. Your perspective shifts. You begin to realize that much of what we value and focus on is insignificant and meaningless in light of eternity.

We often live as if we are going to be on this earth forever. Think of it this way. Let's say you went on vacation and checked into your hotel room, where you planned to stay for a couple of weeks. But you didn't like the appearance of the room, so you called in your own interior decorator. You put a lot of money into it and changed the wallpaper, the curtains, the artwork—the whole room. Then you wanted a bigger television, so you bought an oversized flat screen and had it mounted on the wall. When you went outside, you didn't like the shrubs and the flowers, so you hired a landscaper. You kept making changes to suit yourself. Then you went home.

That's exactly what many of us do today on this earth. We act as if we're going to be here forever. We concentrate on things that seem really important to us at the moment but that ultimately don't last. ❧

1. During your one-month-to-live challenge, what are some of the things you have decided must be a lower priority in your life?

2. What things of greater value do you now plan to pursue during your remaining time on earth?

⟿ Our focus needs to be redirected to the things that will pass the test of time, and really there are only two: God's Word and people. The Bible says the grass withers and the flowers fade, but the Word of God stands forever (Isaiah 40:8). So when you spend time in God's Word—building your character, becoming more like Christ, learning the values from God's Word, and applying them—that lasts forever. You take that with you into eternity. ⟿

3. What environments or techniques best help you spend time in God's Word?

4. With all the great technology available, why not have a copy of the Bible on your computer, on your iPod, and so on? These tools make it easier than ever to consume God's Word.

The other eternal investment you can make is in people. People live forever in eternity. So anytime you make a difference in the lives of others, it will last forever. That's why relationships are the most important thing in your life.

Too often we focus on things that just don't last. Look at Ecclesiastes 11:7–8: "It is a wonderful thing to be alive! If a person lives to be very old, let him rejoice in every day of life, but let him also remember that eternity is far longer, and that everything down here is futile in comparison" (TLB). No matter how long we live, it will be like only a few seconds in the grand scope of eternity.

5. Think of people in your life who do not know Christ. Pray now for their salvation. None of us wants to leave a loved one behind when we journey to heaven.

What you do with Jesus Christ determines where you spend eternity. What you do with your time, talents, and treasures determines what rewards you get in eternity. Do you remember the board game called The Game of Life? You got to choose your career and lifestyle, and then at the end of the game, there was Reckoning Day when your choices were evaluated. It's not so far from the way we'll be held accountable for our decisions. What you do with your dash of time here on this earth prepares you for eternity. Until you understand the fact that life is preparation for eternity, life won't make sense to you.

6. What in your life now is causing you to think more about the things of earth than the things of heaven?

Enact

Since you're reading this last session in the *One Month to Live Guidebook,* obviously you're still with us!

     God willing, you will live for many, many more months, years, or decades, enjoying life to the fullest, forever changed as you embrace who He has made you to be and your passionate pursuit of its fulfillment.

     This, in a nutshell, is the entire premise of the book [*One Month to Live*]. You have been given an extraordinary gift—your life. You have an exceptional calling—to be the very best *you* God created you to be. Your goal is to unwrap this gift and use all that you've been given in the pursuit of what matters most—loving God and loving other people....

     As we conclude our journey together in these pages, I want to offer you one last word. If I were limited to only one thing that you would take from this book, it would be to ignite and restore passion to your life. If you only had one month to live, you would want to enjoy every single moment as the precious gift it is. And you would want to make every second count toward something meaningful and eternal, something that fulfills your purpose on this earth. The fuel for sustaining the one-month-to-live lifestyle over the long haul is passion.

Nothing great ever happens without passion. The driving force behind all masterful art, all moving music, all classic literature, all powerful drama, all stunning architecture is passion. Passion propels athletes to break records. Passion pushes scientists to discover new cures for diseases. Passion drives us to share the love of God in creative, innovative ways with those around us. Passion is what gives life to life. ❧

1. Who's the most passionate person you know? What do you think fuels his or her passion?

2. How might you use your passions more effectively to fulfill your destiny and advance God's plans on earth?

❧ God intends for us to live passionately. "So love the Lord God with all your passion and prayer and intelligence and energy" (Mark 12:30, MSG). We were made with the capacity for passion because God is a passionate God, and we're made in His image. We're told, "Never be lacking in zeal, but keep your spiritual fervor, serving the Lord" (Romans 12:11). Notice the word "keep"; it tells us that passion is something we can lose. If we don't work at it, the stresses and pressures of life can steal our passion for our families, friends, and careers. ❧

Keeping Passion Burning

❧ In order to keep our passion alive and thriving, we must be sure to include its four key ingredients. The first piece of the passion puzzle is the most important—love. Love is the foundation of a passionate, purposeful life. ❧

3. Why is love such a key component of a passionate life?

❧ The next essential in a passionate life is integrity. While people may define this term in a variety of ways, integrity is simply uniting what we say we believe with the way we live. Just as lust destroys the passion in our lives, so does a lack of integrity. Nothing dilutes our passion more than when we say we believe something but don't live it out. When we say our health is important but we consistently overeat unhealthy foods, we lose integrity. When we say our families are important but we're always working and are never present, we lose heart. When we say we love God as the foundation for our lives but we don't relate to Him on a daily basis, we suffer. Our hearts become divided, and we lose the primary focus of our lives. ❧

4. This is between you and the Lord—are there any areas in your life that lack integrity? If yes, confess them and ask God for power to align what you believe with what you do.

↶ The next element essential to sustaining passion is forgiveness. In each of the four [core principles], forgiveness has emerged in one form or another as a vital part of the one-month-to-live lifestyle. Nothing drains passion quicker than unresolved conflict. Job 5:2 tells us, "Surely resentment destroys the fool, and jealousy kills the simple" (NLT). These two—resentment and jealousy—will steal passion quicker than anything else. ↶

5. Do you agree or disagree that unresolved conflict is a significant hindrance to strong passion? Explain why you feel this way.

↶ Finally, we need enthusiasm to maintain our passion in life. The word *enthusiasm* comes from two Greek words: *en* and *theos*. *Theos* is the Greek word for "God," and *en* simply means "in," so literally it means "God within." If you want to live each and every day as if it were your last, then you must focus on your relationship with God. If you struggle with passion in your life, perhaps you aren't cultivating your relationship with Him at the level for which you were designed. ~

6. In your experience, what are the attitudes and actions that make your relation-ship with God sizzle?

7. If you struggle to maintain a close relationship with God, ask people who are more spiritually mature how they keep a dynamic friendship with God.

~ Love. Integrity. Forgiveness. Enthusiasm. *Life.* The passionate life, the one life we've been given to live. ~

Examples of a Passionate Life

~ When I look at Jesus' life, I see someone who knew how to live. In fact, Jesus knew how much time He had left. So how did He live when He knew He had one month left on earth? He lived out these four principles that we've looked at. ~

8. List one or more incidents that you recall from Jesus' life that reveal His passion.

❧ When my mom was about the age I am now, she found out that she had cancer, and it wasn't long until she was told she had one month to live. But the beautiful thing was that she had nothing to change. From the day she heard those words, she kept on living the same way. Why? Because she had been living intentionally all along. She'd been loving the people in her life completely. She'd been doing the things she needed to do. She hadn't left things unsaid that she needed to say. So when she found out she had one month left, she was able to continue down the same path. My goal for you and for me is that we will live intentionally so we will have no regrets. I pray that when you and I reach our last day on this earth, we will know that we have lived completely the life we were made for. ❧

Journal Your Life

Based on your study of this session of the guide, record your thoughts related to living like there's no tomorrow. What thoughts do you have now about the rest of your life and the legacy that you will leave behind?

_____

_____

Small Group Discussion

Take a few minutes to review the journey of each group member since you were last together.

1. C. S. Lewis wrote, "If I discover within myself a desire which no experience in this world can satisfy, the most probable explanation is that I was made for another world." Do you ever experience such a desire, one that nothing on earth seems to satisfy? Why do you think we have such feelings?

2. In the Old Testament book of Ecclesiastes it says, "It is a wonderful thing to be alive! If a person lives to be very old, let him rejoice in every day of life, but let him also remember that eternity is far longer, and that everything down here is futile in comparison" (11:7–8, TLB). How would you explain eternity? How should the magnitude of eternity influence how we live each day?

3. What do you think heaven will be like? (See Revelation 21 for insights.)

4. The book *One Month to Live* says, "If we want to experience heaven, then we must live each moment here on earth prepared for eternity. You're not really ready to live until you're ready to die." What do you think is meant by the last sentence?

5. If someone stopped you on the street and asked, "Are you ready to die?" what would your answer be?

6. How should the fact that only *God's Word* and *people* will last forever influence our attitudes and actions during our time on earth?

7. In *One Month to Live* we read, "If I were limited to only one thing that you would take from this book, it would be to ignite and restore passion to your life." What are some ways to ensure that you remain passionate about fulfilling God's plan for your life?

8. As this group ends, take a few minutes to tell one another what changes have occurred in your life since this study began.

9. Take turns sharing—what would you really appreciate prayer for in the coming weeks?

Wrap up with prayer for one another.

Next?

In the days ahead, continue to visit www.OneMonthToLive.com to learn more about how to live your life to the fullest.

Conclusion

Congratulations for completing this companion guide to *One Month to Live*! We trust that your life will not be the same, and that from this day forward, you will reap the spiritual benefits of living passionately while completing the plan God has crafted just for you.

We urge you to continue to study and apply the principles expressed in both the book *One Month to Live* and this guide. The one-month-to-live challenge is only the beginning! As life changing as a thirty-day commitment to clarify your focus can be, for most of us, God has granted a whole lot more of life to live! That means ongoing challenges to stay on target and continually growing in our obedience to God. Our own sins and weaknesses, as well as the plots of our Enemy, will surely drag us down if we do not maintain our vigilance in applying what we've learned.

We encourage you to seek daily encouragement and ideas for all aspects of your life from our Web site www.OneMonthToLive.com. Let us know how your journey is going—we would love to hear from you.

God bless you in all the days He has given you to enjoy this incredible adventure!

Kerry   Chris

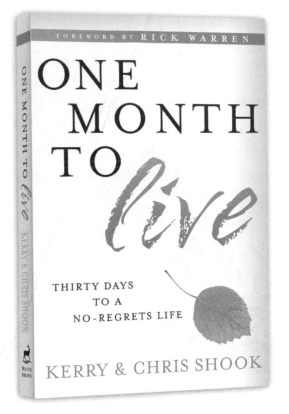

About the Authors

Kerry and Chris Shook founded Fellowship of The Woodlands in 1993 with eight people. Since then, the church has grown to more than fifteen thousand people, becoming one of the largest and most influential churches in America. Its main campus is in The Woodlands, outside of Houston, Texas.

Striving to eliminate the barriers that keep people from experiencing a relationship with Jesus Christ, Kerry and Chris believe that church should be engaging and life changing. They have touched thousands of under-resourced people locally and in countries around the world through the missions and ministries of Fellowship of The Woodlands.

Their weekly television program is broadcast to millions of viewers. It can be seen in all fifty states and more than two hundred countries worldwide.

Kerry and Chris have been married for nearly twenty-five years and have four children.